The Power Chicks' Guide to Boston

In their own words

Table of Contents

Acknowledgements

In the year it has taken to write this book, I have incurred debts among many friends, some old, some new, and to all, I am grateful.

The idea for a guide book addressed to women who aspire to a professional career came from two of my account directors, one a woman and the other, ironically, a man — Lisa Mansdorf Pollack and Paul Jean, who were impressed by the panorama of questions asked by young women and suggested that young women might benefit from a book that provided advice from women who had successfully traveled in Boston's civic, charitable and business communities.

Throughout the process of interviewing and writing, many others have contributed selflessly, especially colleagues in my office, and in particular Diana Pisciotta, John Henning, Roberta Shaw, Terence Burke, and also Nicole Russell, without whose skills at organization this project long since would have foundered.

Kristie DiSalvo of Denterlein Worldwide was patient with my procrastination and indefatigable in editing the manuscript, always making it better. An award-winning reporter in Virginia and former writer for the *Banker & Tradesman* in Boston, she brought to the text not only an intimate knowledge of the nuances of split infinitives and predicate nominatives, but also a subtle sensitivity to the issues faced by young women.

I am indebted, too, to Lisa Mansdorf Pollack, whose studies on women's issues at Brandeis and whose service as a press secretary to Mayor Thomas M. Menino enabled her to provide valuable insights into the needs of women generally, but especially in Boston.

I will be always grateful to many others outside of the office. A contributor to the manuscript was one of Boston's favorite doyennes, the irrepressible Nancy Gaines, who knows a thing or two about writing, about women and about Boston. Helping me fathom the refinements of Boston's charitable community was one of Boston's most refined and charitable citizens, Robin Brown. When I had questions about Boston society, I went to the people who know the stories behind the stories, and among them were Bill Brett of the *Boston Globe*, Dana Bisbee, formerly of the *Boston Herald*, and that clever character from the *Improper Bostonian*, Jonathan Soroff.

I draw strength from the inner circle of women in my life who have taught me that what is truly essential transcends the concept of power. For this and more, I love Faith Tracy, Jennifer Rando, Judy Glasser, Estie Rappaport, Karen Reiber, and Christine Shane.

And finally, for a comfort in the knowledge that I can have a career and a family, too, I thank my son, John Patrick Thomas, and my husband, Jack Thomas. Every night when I arrive home from work to their love, their loyalty and their laughter, I am reminded of the goodness of life.

About the Author

As founder of Denterlein Worldwide Public Affairs, Geri Denterlein leads a growing company that specializes in strategic communications and is known for its successful public policy campaigns, crisis communications work, and healthcare consulting. Drawing on more than 25 years of experience in media, government and business, she provides executive level communications and public relations counsel to businesses, nonprofits, colleges and healthcare organizations.

Prior to serving as a consultant, Geri was editorial director at WBZ television and radio, where she was responsible for the station's government and community outreach and also for the writing and on-air delivery of editorials and political analysis. She also was featured regularly on WBZ-AM with a "State House Update." Geri's government service includes terms as communication director for the departments of Mental Health and Retardation and also as an associate press secretary to former Gov. Michael S. Dukakis.

Geri has written columns for or been featured in articles published in the *Boston Globe, Boston Herald, Women's Business, Boston Business Journal* and *Inc. Magazine*. She serves on numerous civic and nonprofit boards including, MassINC, A Better City and WGBH's Corporate Executive Council. She is a trustee of the Massachusetts Taxpayers Foundation and Vice Chair of the Board of Directors of the American Red Cross of Massachusetts Bay. Geri has been honored by the Boston Chamber of Commerce with the Pinnacle Award for Achievement in Management.

She holds a Bachelor of Science degree from the University of Cincinnati and a Master of Public Administration from Harvard's Kennedy School of Government.

Geri lives in Cambridge, with her husband, writer Jack Thomas, and their son, John Patrick Thomas.

Preface

Years ago, when I was Editorial Director at WBZ-TV Channel 4 in Boston, I assumed that the key to success was keeping long hours, arriving early at the office and staying late. After all, that was how good girls got promoted, right?

Every day, I pored through a stack of newspapers, national, regional, local, and even the many trade publications that cater to the broadcast industry. I studied techniques to improve my skills at interviewing, and I worked with photographers to learn the subtleties in the visual art of television production. I was dedicated, all right. Boy, was I dedicated!

Then one day my boss, General Manager John Spinola, stopped by my desk while I was engrossed in some arcane appraisal of the future of the communications industry. "Geri, you really keep your nose to the grindstone," he said, "but if all you do is keep your nose to the grindstone, all you get is a shiny nose."

Thanks, boss. Those words became my epiphany.

I began to think outside the box of conventional rules and also outside the office. I developed contacts around town, in government, business, society, sports, philanthropy and especially in the news media: radio, television, magazines, and newspapers. At first it was by telephone or by chance encounters at parties, business meetings or social events. But I began to follow up with invitations to meetings, one on one. I set up breakfasts at the Four Seasons Hotel, lunches at Locke-Ober, and drinks after work at restaurants that I knew were not so noisy as to make conversation difficult. After all, I wasn't there for the music.

What I learned, thanks to my boss, was a primary strategy in promoting my employer and in selling myself — get out of the office.

Young professional women today are not as naïve as I was. They recognize that social and civic involvement have tangible rewards in the form of more business, broader knowledge and better friends.

For centuries, women have been expected to know their place. In New England, the standard was set in 1638 when Anne Hutchinson was banished from Boston for being assertive. Three centuries went by and as late as the 1960s, women were banned from the main dining room at Locke-Ober, which now is owned, ironically, by a woman, Lydia Shire. If our mothers were condemned for being outspoken or — Horrors! — aggressive, young women today know that if they are not outgoing and outspoken, they cannot hope to outrun and outperform the competition.

Peculiarly Boston

Times have changed and we are grateful that Boston women are no longer what Gilbert and Sullivan called diffident, modest and shy. Certainly, there is no shortage of role models in our city, where women have been elevated to the leadership of institutions once considered male citadels — banks, businesses, governments, universities, hospitals, news media and law enforcement agencies.

In fact, Boston is such a grand city that many people want to live here. As a result, the marketplace is crowded and competition in the workplace is keen and sometimes cutthroat.

Among the many things for which Boston can take credit is this — it is a matter of pride in Boston for business leaders to support community and charity events, to be seen as caring. Benevolence in the marketplace is worth the investment for two reasons: first, because it's the right thing to do and, second, because it's also good for business.

In mercantile New York, the currency of power may be money. In Los Angeles, it may be notoriety and, of course, good looks. But in Boston, in this ineffably Puritan City on a Hill, it's a characteristic among people of influence that they also give back, and what happens as a result? They reap even greater rewards.

It may not seem fair, but being great at your job may not be enough to elevate you into the corridors of power. In Boston, to do well, you have to do good works too, and that often requires a willingness to extend the workday past the traditional 5 PM quitting time and into the evening hours.

In the 25 years I've been active in the Boston public arena, young women have asked me to share with them the tips and tricks of the trade. But increasingly, their questions are not limited merely to the traditional goals of success in business or public affairs. They also want to know how to develop power in Boston in the peculiar triangle of profession, community and social life. They wonder about the merits of a mentor, and if so, who and how do they find her? Even if they're willing to put in those extra hours after work, how do they find the time? How do they engender invitations to the parties and social events of consequence? And especially, once there, how do they work a dinner, cocktail party or other soiree?

Naming Names
The Power Chicks' Guide to Boston: In their own words provides the answers. Culling from my own public speeches and presentations, from focus groups of young women, and from interviews with leading executive women, not to mention informal gabfests, I've come up with a primer on how to navigate the circles of power in Boston.

You'll hear young women ask the questions, and then you can sit at the knees of the gray hairs — dubbed with due deference,

of course — the grande dames of Boston, as they delve into
their experience to provide guidance for the next generation of
women. One section is devoted to practical advice from a
cadre of successful women who've been through the fire
and rain.

Every detail matters — what business groups you belong to,
which events you attend, the charities you support, the lunch
guests you entertain and, in the matter of alcohol, when,
where, what and how much and — the most sobering question
— whether to drink at all.

Nothing beats talent, charm and diligence in elbowing for
power and recognition, but pluck has its place, too, and *The
Power Chicks' Guide to Boston: In their own words* lays out an
array of strategies with which an up-and-coming professional
woman can fortify herself for the campaigns ahead.

Before we go any further, a confession of sorts about the phrase
"power chicks." I know that it may offend some people, and
indeed, as a lifelong feminist, I too have bristled at the term
"chick." But I learned something in our focus groups. Someone
mentioned "chick lit," a term popular among younger women to
define literature written for them, and after a spirited discussion,
women in our focus group accepted "power chick" as a simple,
vivid and inoffensive term to describe a class of women we
admire who are successful, influential, socially conscious and
essential to us as teachers.

The guide is based on my own experiences and also upon
those of some exceptional Boston women, whose names you
know, or ought to, and whose faces you recognize, or ought
to. In many ways this guidebook is a group effort. Encouraged
by younger women in my office, I set out initially to expand
upon a speech I had delivered to the Women's Network of
the Boston Chamber of Commerce. That induced some

women to pose follow-up questions, and the responses prompted still more queries. To find the answers, I assembled a focus group of 30-somethings women, conducted dozens of one-on-one interviews with some of the city's most influential women, and communicated with many others by email. The result is this guidebook. Within its covers, a young woman with dreams can find practical advice, sisterly counsel and wisdom accumulated by women who've gone before and whom I admire.

They speak candidly about how to assess your power base, then how to augment it. They tell how to make the most of your natural assets to enhance that base, and how to utilize, to the best advantage, your education, skills, contacts and outreach.

Of the hundreds of annual social-business parties, the guide pinpoints a dozen or so that are "must-attend." It talks directly about the powerful players you want to wine and dine — well, dine if not wine.

On the charitable front, the guide identifies organizations that offer young professionals the opportunity to become leaders. It also provides lists of charitable events according to ticket price. There's also a catalogue of the best spots in Boston for power dining.

Since I began this project, Massachusetts has experienced a significant shift in power at the State House. Deval Patrick, a Chicago native, has become the state's highest ranking elected official. Portrayed during the campaign as an outsider, he won the election on a platform that welcomed into the political process the young and the disaffected, including women. His inauguration, in January of 2007, brought to Massachusetts a wave of excitement and optimism not seen on Beacon Hill for many years.

Goveror Patrick, who has urged charitable and civic organizations to be more welcoming, is changing volunteerism in Massachusetts. For any young professional seeking to expand her network, while at the same time making a difference in the community, this is a propitious time to become involved.

Elevating women to roles of power is an earnest challenge, to be sure, but my goal in this guidebook has been to include humor as well as wisdom. Not everyone should be a CEO, but given that most women, at some point, will find themselves enrolled in the work force, why shouldn't we strive to our greatest potential? As men have known for years, the higher you climb the ladder, the better the view.

To any woman who wants to make it in our city, *The Power Chicks' Guide to Boston: In their own words* is full of fun and useful information. And to all those women who've paved the way for us, we thank you.

Oh, and one other thing — about that grindstone? After I lifted my nose from it, I felt a lot better.

— Geri Denterlein
Boston 2007

Published by Denterlein Worldwide, Boston

Cover concept and design: Resa Blatman
Book concept and design: Gary Stanton and Donna Stepien
Illustrations: Gary Stanton
Layout: Donna Stepien
Typesetting and page makeup: Lake Initiatives

ISBN 978-0-937383-18-2

The Power Chicks' Guide to Boston

In their own words

Geri Denterlein

1. What Is Power?

They are women of power, and you see them everywhere —
in elevators and coffee shops, alighting from cabs or dining
at Boston's best restaurants. They are dressed in sleek business
suits and high heels, and often there's a BlackBerry within reach
of their perfectly manicured nails. There's a look about them,
too, of pure determination and, even though they may be
running nonstop from one meeting to the next, there's an air
of grace, too.

They are Boston's Power Chicks. They know what to say.
They know when to say it. They know how to convince
members of an executive board to change course. They also
know — or at least give the appearance that they know — the
secrets to balancing work, home and a leadership role in their
community. They strive not only to be successful professionally,
but also to make a mark on their city.

Power is clout, but it can be subtle, too. The women I spoke
to all agree that power is getting people to want to do what
you want them to do —some action that benefits you, your
company, your organization or your community.

Andrea Kramer, a lawyer at Sullivan Weinstein & McQuay,
with a pedigree that includes Wellesley College and Harvard
Law School, underscores the point. "Sure, power is making
things happen, but it's also having a say in what happens," she
says. "So many important decisions that influence what goes on
are made in collaboration with other people."

What are some of the personality traits common in powerful
women? Ambition and passion. How have these women risen
through the ranks? Well, few of them have followed the same
road to the top.

Successful women do not set out on a career based on a
pretension. While it may take time to ascertain her strengths and

passions, a young woman must follow her inner voice. She cannot take pleasure in the perks of power attained by being someone she is not.

"Chart your own course," says Joyce Murphy, vice chancellor and chief operating officer of University of Massachusetts Medical School/ Commonwealth Medicine. "If you follow your heart, you will be successful. If you try to make yourself into a round peg for a square hole, it won't feel right and ultimately will probably not bring success. This is not to say, however, that you should not stretch yourself and try things that may not seem perfect. It is often exactly these experiences where we will succeed and our most valuable lessons are learned."

The women who have contributed to the shaping of this old Brahmin town all recognize the symbiotic value of being true to oneself in both professional and civic involvement. They have mastered the art of being powerful by making a difference, by spreading their sphere of influence. In Boston, their names are easily recognizable: Anne Finucane, president, Northeast, Bank of America, Bain & Company Chair Orit Gadiesh, Regina Pisa, chair and managing partner of Goodwin Procter LLP, Cheryl Cronin, who recently left Brown Rudnick to start her own firm, and Cathy Minehan, who served as president of the Federal Reserve Bank of Boston for 13 years, until her retirement in 2007.

And whoever said that women aren't good at finance and technology hasn't met the powerful women who work in the region's most prestigious companies, including, Donna Cupelo, region president of Massachusetts and Rhode Island for Verizon, Karen Kruck, senior vice president of State Street Corporation, Maura Banta, regional manager of corporate community relations for IBM's Boston office, and Sheryl Marshall, vice president at Credit Suisse.

Other women, as leaders of prestigious universities in Greater Boston, influence the character of our city and, at the same time, motivate the young women and men of the next generation. You've read about them, too: Susan Hockfield, president of MIT, Kay Sloan, president of MassArt, Jackie Jenkins-Scott, president of Wheelock College, Gloria Larson, president of Bentley College, Kim Bottomly, president of Wellesley College, and Drew Gilpin Faust, who recently became the 28th president of Harvard. There is also Margaret McKenna, who led Lesley University for 22 years and is now president of the Wal-Mart Foundation.

Some of Boston's luminaries are involved in the highest levels of healthcare, one of Massachusetts' most renowned industries. Sandra Fenwick, chief operating officer of Children's Hospital Boston, has been called one of the hospital's most visible leaders in its history. And, as president and CEO of Neighborhood Health Plan, Deborah Enos leads one of the health insurance companies critical to the success of the state's health reform efforts. Boston's healthcare leaders also include Ellen Zane, president and CEO of Tufts-New England Medical Center, Elaine Ullian, president and CEO of Boston Medical Center, Jeanette Clough, President and CEO of Mount Auburn Hospital, Fay Donahue, president and CEO of Delta Dental of Massachusetts, Dolores Mitchell, executive director of the Commonwealth of Massachusetts Group Insurance Commission, Mary Lou Buyse, president of the Massachusetts Association of Health Plans and Elizabeth Pattullo, president and CEO of Beacon Health Strategies.

Sometimes Power Chicks prefer to maintain a lower profile, although they make their mark by their money. We've all heard about the Million Dollar Man, but when you see an "Anonymous" at the top of the donor list, it may well be Boston's Billion Dollar Woman, $13 billion to be exact — Fidelity's Abby Johnson, whose appetite for privacy cannot camouflage her extraordinary generosity to Boston.

Then there are the women in the media whose power flows from the pen, keyboard or camera. Although *Boston Globe* Executive Editor Helen Donovan operates under the radar and, therefore, rarely makes the power lists, she exerts great influence. Vicki Donlan, publisher of *Women's Business*, has done more to shine the spotlight on successful business women than anyone else in this town. Wendy Semonian, publisher of the *Improper Bostonian*, is a force as well. Broadcast executive Julie Kahn, vice president of Entercom Boston, was recently the only Bostonian to make the cut for *Radio Ink Magazine*'s ranking of the "50 Most Influential Women in Radio."

Writers are a breed apart from the rest of us, and notable for their power quotient. News gals like Joan Vennocchi, Renee Loth, Margery Eagan, and Ellen Goodman wield extraordinary influence. The *Boston Herald*'s "Inside Track" girls, Gayle Fee and Laura Raposa, may be powerful for the fear they engender, but nevertheless, they are a "must read" for anyone who wants talking points on Boston's sports and celebrity gossip. Television personalities, such as Janet Wu, Liz Walker, Liz Brunner, Susan Warnick, Emily Rooney, Lisa Hughes and anchor Natalie Jacobson, who retired in 2007 after a 35 year career as Boston's most influential news anchor, are deeply embedded in the city's circle of charities. For ex-news gals Mary Jo Meisner and Suzanne Bates, journalism proved to be a NASA-like platform to launch successful careers in business. The difference between them and the rest of us working women is that they have, by virtue of their news organizations, a ready made podium.

Media jobs and white collar careers are not the only means to get a seat at the table. Unions have cultivated political power on the Hill and in the Hall. Kathy Casavant, treasurer of the Massachusetts AFL-CIO, Celia Wcislo, president of SEIU Local 2020, and Janice Loux, president of Unite Here Local 26, which represents hotel and restaurant workers, have a voice in the debate about how best to move working people up the economic ladder.

There is also a category we'll call the rich wives' club, whose members join with financially endowed divorcees, heiresses, and assorted celebrities, many of whom bestow blessings on local charities by contributing time and a lot of money. Many once worked in the professional world, but now devote their energy to charitable causes. In their ability to organize and to prop up charities, these women wield influence and engender the city's admiration and gratitude.

The wives of owners and players of Boston's beloved sports teams add sparkle to dozens of charitable events each year.

There are women who derive power by virtue of their husbands and families, but who use the role to make an impression of their own. Teresa Heinz Kerry devotes time and cash to national causes and to charities in Pittsburgh as well as in Boston. Angela Menino and Diane Patrick lend their names and countless hours of work to dozens of charitable causes. Victoria Kennedy and Caroline Kennedy Schlossberg enhance the legacy of the family whose name is synonymous with public service.

Women are certainly making an impact in politics, and often with subtle sweetness.

Massachusetts' women are in good company at the highest levels of government, including Lisa Signori, chief financial officer for the City of Boston, Leslie Kirwan, Massachusetts' Secretary of Administration and Finance, and Katherine Craven, executive director of the Massachusetts School Building Authority.

In 2007, women celebrated when Martha Coakley won the Attorney General race and Therese Murray succeeded Robert

Travaglini to become the first woman to serve as president of the Massachusetts Senate. At a press conference, Senator Murray referred to the election of Martha Coakley and the unanimous vote by which Maureen Feeney became the second woman to serve as president of the Boston City Council.

"The election of the three of us," she said, "demonstrates that in 2007, gender was no longer an issue in choosing government leaders."

The Favor Bank

We can learn a thing or two from men who know about power. Take Bob Popeo, for instance, one of Boston's top power players and chairman of the law firm Mintz, Levin, Cohn, Ferris, Glovsky and Popeo.

"There is no question that power is renewable," he said in a 2001 interview with *Boston Business Forward* magazine. "If your influence is dependent upon a particular administration or particular individuals who you had networked with, then that influence is going to have a shelf life that is not going to sustain you for a very long period of time. Influence is really developed by understanding what issues drive the community, who are the people who drive those issues, how they will influence the greater good of the Commonwealth, and how you make those things happen."

How often you can revitalize your status may depend upon your standing in what Bob calls the "Boston Favor Bank." It's an imaginary institution where favors are deposited, and then they are repaid and, sometimes, they are called in.

Anyone who knows Bob Popeo knows that the favors in his Favor Bank, done and repaid, are huge.

For the rest of us mere mortals, let's just apply the concept. It's important to recognize that there are always good deeds that can be deposited into your Favor Bank — i.e., meeting with a college student who is looking for a job, inviting a colleague to a professional event, or making a flattering introduction.

Each year, my company holds a retreat during which outside speakers offer perspectives on business. One of Boston's preeminent lawyers, Mark Robinson, a partner at Bingham McCutchen, brought the punch home to our business. "Never meet with anyone in the business world without first thinking, what can I do for them. Ask yourself: Is there an introduction I could make, information I could provide or an opportunity I could offer?" Think about every relationship you have, social as well as business. There is always something you can do for someone else.

The advantage of a Favor Bank was among the most important lessons learned along her formidable career path, says Rosabeth Moss Kanter of Harvard Business School. "Knowing what other people need and helping them get it is a better way to lead than thinking about one's own needs. Being attuned to others and generous to them is the best form of enlightened self-interest."

All power sectors have their own Favor Banks. In this city, the president of the imaginary Favor Bank is Jack Connors, Boston's ultimate powerbroker. Founder of the advertising agency Hill | Holliday and chairman of Partners HealthCare, Jack has mastered the art of good deeds.

Some have been well published, but many others not at all.

None of this is done because he expects payback, but rather because he wants the favor to be paid forward and for business leaders to gild their power with good works. He explains his proclivity to charity by paraphrasing the Book of Luke: "To whom much is given, much is required."

Described by Steve Bailey of the *Boston Globe* as "the face of corporate leadership" whose influence has been predicated on a "network of relationships unparalleled in Boston," Jack never lets go of his marketing skills. When he made a multi-million dollar gift to Brigham and Women's Hospital in honor of his mother, he timed the release for the news to be published on Mother's Day.

When he sold his company Hill | Holliday to the Interpublic Group at a price of more than $100 million, he hired me to handle the publicity. It was a plum assignment. Although I had known Jack for years through business and charitable circles, I had not worked for him nor did I know him well. However, we forged a fast friendship in the whirlwind days surrounding the sale. Some time later, while I was weighing the wisdom of starting my own business, I sought his counsel.

He suggested we meet for a walk on a Sunday morning. He let me talk about my concerns of being on my own in the corporate world and, of course, my fear of failure. After all, I had prepared myself to be a journalist, not a business woman. In the end, he expressed his philosophy of business, and his confidence in me. I left with the conviction I needed to make the leap.

Mark that down as a deposit in my Favor Bank.

Why You Should Care
For better or worse, most of us want to be associated with people who are perceived as successful and powerful. Like it or not, many women will work outside the home for much of their adult life. Why not make the most of those years in the workplace? Why not transform the experience into an opportunity to make a difference?

At the risk of sounding like an infomercial, think of yourself as a commodity. You want to stand out, to be noticed. You need good display. Then, you have to be reliable, effective, durable and consistent.

Enhancing your personal brand makes you more interesting, more authoritative and a finer corporate citizen. Most women who become power players cultivate certain styles and skills that make them more effective communicators, business executives and individuals. Few of us are natural born leaders. Those who lead do so by cultivating personal style and persuasive skills, and these can be learned.

KAREN KAPLAN On: Success
Karen Kaplan began her career as a receptionist to Jack Connors, then president of Hill | Holliday. As she progressed through the ranks, Karen knew that if she accomplished each task by investing more time and effort than her colleagues, success would follow. Twenty-five years later, the president's office is now her own.

Successful people never coast because they know you only coast one way and that's downhill. No matter who you are and how hard you work, you always need to keep your eyes wide open. Everyone is born with a natural curiosity – retain it. Successful people are inspired not by how much they know but by how much they don't know. They listen to their clients and employees, they stay on top of emerging trends, and they give change a big, warm hug. They know they can always be better and do better. Our success is measured by our ability to embrace and manage change.

2. Assess Your Power Tools

In preparation for this guidebook, I did first what any meticulous woman in marketing would do — research. I brought together a focus group of 20 women, average age 32, from professions including law, government, arts, and real estate. I asked them to discuss the business world, success and failure for women, their fantasies and fears.

We debated which Boston organizations, institutions, boards, clubs — even restaurants — equaled power in their minds. Who, what and where did they want to be in 10 years? In 20 years? What were the barriers? What did they need to achieve their goals?

We talked about style and skills, natural and learned — taken together, an inventory of power tools. Thoughts on style included leadership; the ability to communicate effectively; appearance; how to work a room; how to listen well; and how to make and keep connections. Skills included education, languages, sports and outreach.

It was obvious that younger women today are blessed with an assurance that comes from having lived with and watched one or two generations of women in the workforce. Not that young women have it all figured out, not by a long shot, for they are still asking a question that nagged their mothers and grandmothers: Is it possible to have a high-powered career and a family, too? Young women in the mom circle are confident that, with the right tools, they can manage both a career and a home.

The Gen X and Gen Y generations also have the advantage over their mothers in that revolutionary resource, the Internet. A generation ago, we did our fact-finding by telephone. We prepared for a meeting, a conference or a working social event by talking to colleagues and friends. It was tedious, time consuming and, by comparison, neither thorough nor effective.

Today, thanks to the Internet, that kind of research is so easy that young women no longer have an excuse for arriving unprepared at a working event. Thanks, Google!

The focus group came to a consensus on the common qualities of a leader — confidence, creativity, diligence, reliability and diplomacy. The barriers: intimidations in the business world, a lack of money and time and, as one 29-year-old put it, the need for "connections, connections, connections!"

But before a Power Chick focuses on how to improve, she assesses what she's got.

Take Inventory

Imagine if Boston's most powerful women carried tool kits in their purses and made a quick accounting on their way out the door each morning. The inventory might go something like this: Self-confidence? Check. Flawless public speaking? Check. Proven ability to take risks and negotiate with colleagues? Check, check, check.

What would yours include?

Not every skill comes naturally. In fact, many successful women have spent years honing the tools in their kit. Not sure how you stack up? Here's a simple self-assessment that will indicate which of your skills may need fine tuning and which may yet be awaiting discovery. Once you have a better idea of where you rank, I'll point you to corresponding chapters that can help.

For each set of questions, give yourself 0-3 points.
0 — Never
1 — Rarely
2 — Most of the time
3 — Always

The Big Picture

____ I know with confidence that I dress appropriately for business and social occasions.

____ I am deft enough at conversation to talk about my accomplishments without being boastful.

____ When I speak and write, I am attentive to rules of grammar.

____ I embrace my individuality, and I am comfortable sharing who I am.

____ When I meet someone, I can describe my professional career in 30 seconds or less.

____ As part of my networking strategy, I am involved in at least two organizations in the following fields: professional, political, personal or charitable.

____ I talk about work in my business and social circles.

____ I recognize when individuals "overlap" in the various spheres, and I work to strengthen my relationships with them.

If you scored fewer than 21 points, you may have trouble seeing the bigger picture. See Chapter 3 for more tips.

Your Brand

____ I read the newspaper everyday, even the sports pages, and I am conversant on the hot topics of the day.

____ Each month, I attend at least two business, trade or civic events.

____ Before each event, I do my homework. I know who will be there, and I research the people I hope to meet.

____ I always arrive on time, and I use the cocktail portion of the event to network.

____ After each event, I follow up with one or two new contacts by personal note or by email, sometimes with an invitation to coffee or lunch.

____ I send relevant newspaper articles to new acquaintances.

____ My database of contacts also includes their personal interests and a record of follow up notes.

____ My boss is supportive of my involvement in civic and charitable organizations.

____ I have worked on public speaking skills so that I appear polished and confident at business meetings.

Did you score fewer than 24 points? Sounds like you know where to be, but not what to do after you leave an event. Check out Chapters 4 and 5 for ideas on how to maintain your connections.

Power Chicks in Training

____ I am a good listener.

____ When my boss bestows a compliment, I accept it graciously.

____ I know how to make a persuasive point in meetings.

____ Mistakes don't consume me.

_____ I am aware of organizations that appreciate sweat equity as well as cash donations.

_____ I don't just belong in name to organizations and boards. When something is needed, I volunteer.

_____ When I find an organization that supports my interests, I know how to become involved.

_____ I leverage the support of my company in civic engagement.

You may be involved, but do you know how to use your connections to reach the next level? If you scored 21 points or fewer, read Chapters 6 and 7 for more tips.

Dispel the Myths

Before you move on, take a moment to slay the myth dragon. You may be carrying around preconceived — and incorrect — notions about what it takes to succeed. Here are a few of the common issues that tend to hold young women back:

MYTH #1: Working long hours will guarantee success

Fourteen hour days, eating three meals a day at your desk, and barely noticing what's happening outside of your office door — to many women, it's all part of getting ahead. Work hard and you'll be rewarded, or at least that's what we're told.

But many young women don't realize that they're missing half of the game. Yes, you must work hard. Yes, you must know your profession. But unless you break free of that desk and begin creating a circle of contacts outside the office, your efforts will fall flat. Hard work alone will not make you a Power Chick.

For Grace Fey, now executive vice president of Frontier Capital Management Company, this myth came crashing down in 1986. She had been with an investment firm for six years, generated excellent financial returns, shown an ability to bring in new clients, and felt that she was a real team player in terms of interacting and helping the partners manage the firm. Based on her performance, she asked the senior partner for a larger equity stake during her review.

"To my shock, he told me that, in his opinion, I did not have the right credentials — to him, a Harvard MBA — and for a woman, he thought I was making enough money," says Grace. "I spent the next several weeks upset and pondering my choices. I decided that I needed to move on. It took me about six months to find something great and I have never looked back."

MYTH #2: Those who succeed are Boston's Insiders
Gov. Patrick is one of many so-called outsiders who have proven that the bluebloods aren't the only brokers with connections in Boston these days. Gloria Larson, the new president of Bentley College, ranked No.1 on *Boston Magazine*'s list of most powerful women in 2003. Margaret H. Marshall, chief justice of the Massachusetts Supreme Judicial Court, and many others have shown us that ambition, a strong work ethic and a commitment to the community can trump the DNA credentials so cherished by descendants of the Mayflower.

MYTH #3: I'm too young for nonprofit board involvement
Wrong — youth is a premium. The city's cultural, civic and social institutions are starving for new blood, especially with the dwindling population of the city and its immediate environs. High housing costs in Boston have stifled the earlier migration of the young, smart and restless. The population, especially those likely to help nonprofit groups (wealthy empty nesters, for instance) is aging.

Now, I'm from the South, so of course, I noticed that people here have a colder affect. But when you take a closer look, it's really just the opposite. I found Boston wonderfully welcoming. It's an invigorating place to live. We need to be bolder about telling the story of the strengths of the region.

MYTH #4: I can't afford to get involved in the civic/charitable circles

Most of the important social/cultural groups in the area assess lower membership fees for young people, or for those willing to do some volunteer work. Civic duties, meanwhile, usually don't cost a penny, unless you're paying out of pocket for those campaign signs held high at the rotary. Most government offices and candidates wish they could pay you. Volunteerism is golden.

MYTH #5: Political decisions happen only in government

For women interested in careers in government, it's obvious that hiring and firing decisions are made because of politics. A new administration can clear an entire floor. What many people don't realize is that the small "p" of politics plays a role in business as well. If your friend or mentor gets promoted, think about how it could help you. Conversely, if your boss is on the outs, it will affect you. If you find yourself caught up in someone else's political drama, see it for what it is. Do not let someone else's bump in the road affect your self-confidence.

MYTH #6: If I haven't settled on a career by 29, I'm sunk

Another misconception, perhaps a holdover from The Greatest

Generation, is that you must follow one career path from graduation to retirement in order to reach your full power quotient. One woman told me of her struggle with this dilemma. A recent college graduate, she knew two things for sure — she loved politics and social causes. Her friends headed off to graduate school, focused on the traditional white collar jobs, while she searched for a professional calling. She wavered between law and medicine. If she could just find the answer, success would come naturally — or so she thought.

Her first job in politics launched a series of opportunities, each one building on the skills and status of the one before. After dabbling in a few careers and taking at least two major risks, she found success on her own terms. She now runs a thriving business, one that has tripled in size during the past three years alone. She looks back on her 20s quite differently.

"I used to worry a lot about not being a doctor, lawyer or Indian Chief. I had lots of passion, but my imagined 'perfect career' changed every few months. I put a lot of pressure on myself because I wanted to be something so badly," she says. "I wish I knew that was okay. The challenge of figuring things out can be more difficult for some than others, but it doesn't mean that you're doomed to a life of aimless wandering in the wilderness. Eventually, for me, things became much clearer. As you learn more about yourself, you find things to build on."

MYTH #7: Graduate degrees are a necessary ingredient for professional success

Everyone seems to have a graduate degree, and perhaps because they are so common, they are no longer a ticket to the top — even if the degree is from an Ivy League university. Many young professional women struggle with whether to pursue a master's degree, sometimes spending years weighing the investment. First, ask yourself two questions: Do I need it to pursue my profession? If I don't need it professionally, do I need it personally?

I wish I knew at age 25-30 that we don't have to do it all now, and how to sort out the urgent from the non-urgent. I had such a sense of urgency about everything in the earlier years of my career. As a result, I was probably less patient, less tolerant and more demanding. I wish I knew then that time can be a friend and an enemy and most often we make it one or the other. One can take the time to make change in a more thoughtful fashion – the results are better and most often the urgency is not as crucial as we perceive. When it is urgent, act accordingly, otherwise, patience and pacing make a huge difference in the outcome.

In deciding whether or not to attend graduate school, age can be a factor. If you're already in a job that affords many opportunities, don't feel pressured to make the leap — particularly if you are in your 30s. If you haven't had children, you're probably thinking about it, and in some cases this new focus could mean setbacks at work. If you take time out for graduate school, you're losing time in the job force and the momentum of contributing at a greater level than you did in your 20s. An advanced degree can build confidence, but don't think that, by virtue of the degree alone, you'll carry more sway. It's one more tool in your kit. And, about that Ivy League education, don't labor under the illusion that every successful person has one.

MYTH #8: It's essential always to have consensus

You know the stereotype: Female managers won't move forward until they have total buy-in from their team, while men, on the other hand, are much more realistic. Of course, this is a generalization. However, some women do feel pressured to have everyone on their side.

LIZ LEVIN On: Thinking outside the box

As a woman in a predominantly male engineering firm I learned early that to be and do something significant, I had to develop skills in areas that were markets for our business and that the guys weren't that interested in pursuing. I learned to do environmental projects and permitting when the engineers wanted to design pipes; I learned to build coalitions of support for projects, which the guys couldn't do; and I learned to do multidisciplinary problem solving while the guys were generally better in their own specific fields. The talents I developed out of necessity were extraordinarily helpful to the companies I worked for and carved out new possibilities for their business. Success wasn't guaranteed by hard work. However, it was made possible by being smart about the work that one does and taking risks to do new things and to use skills not typical in the industry.

Deborah Jackson, CEO of the American Red Cross of Massachusetts Bay tells of a time in a previous job, when she was trying to execute an important new strategy, but she was, in her words, stumped and stuck because she didn't have the support. A mentor said that she was focusing too much on those who didn't support the new direction, Deborah recalls, and not enough on finding allies.

"I wanted everyone on board, so as I encountered resistance, it baffled and frustrated me," Deborah remembers. Later, she came to understand that just because an idea is right, doesn't mean that everyone will get behind it. "Sometimes the naysayers truly disagree with an idea, and other times, they need to be heard and communicated with differently. But in the end, you must build a critical mass of support by aligning those who share your vision and ideas."

MYTH #9: Cream rises to the top

They say cream rises to the top, but that doesn't mean that the best people always do. Connections and political acumen trump the cream consistently. You have to work hard, but it's also critical to take time to do other things. Volunteer on a board or become involved in an organization through which you might meet other people.

3. Sharpen Your Power Tools

Now that you have erased the myths and taken that uncompromising look at your natural assets, special skills, education and experience, evaluate what you can accentuate and determine how you can eliminate the negatives. You know which power tools are at your disposal, so it's time to build to the next level. It's time to come up with a plan.

Imagine in this quest for power that you are a political candidate. Before you develop or sharpen a strategy, you must first take a closer look at the four circles of your life. In each sphere, at least one avenue can help you achieve influence. The goal for all aspiring Power Chicks should be involvement in one or two activities in at least two of the four areas. For example:

Understand how the four spheres of your life intersect. Start to recognize people who play a role in two or more of the sets. These are the people who are likely to be your strongest allies in your professional development.

CIRCLE NO. 1: Professional

Trade groups or professional organizations are a natural outlet for leadership opportunities. Talk to someone in the organization's leadership — most institutions are trying to build membership, so it's in their best interest to spend time with you.

Also, look at your job as a platform. What connections do you have through work that you could leverage in a professional organization? Ask the higher-ups in your office to recommend professional groups that you might join. They will know which organizations are relevant to your industry, and which ones are merely window dressing

CIRCLE NO. 2: Political

Find a candidate or cause that you can embrace. Not only will you get to know the city, but you could end up with some meaningful contacts, particularly if your candidate wins the election. There is no better way to network and meet people than by joining a campaign.

You'll quickly recognize names, the idea-people and the big contributors. But remember, seeking out the power players should not be a No.1 concern when deciding where to volunteer. It's more important to support someone for whom you can vote on Election Day. You can become involved, too, by campaigning for political initiatives such as petition drives, referenda and local issues.

CIRCLE NO. 3: Personal

Consider the personal obligations and pleasures in your life and ask youself if you can become more deeply involved. Faith-based organizations not only feed your soul, but they also provide an opportunity to meet people on an informal basis. Most of these organizations rely on volunteers, many of whom will be leaders at the forefront in the business community as well. The local historical society or library may plan interesting activities, and for women with families, activities at your child's school can be a great way to expand your network. Think the PTA or your son's or daughter's soccer team. Relationships born of values and shared interest can be the strongest and often lead to loyal alliances in business.

CIRCLE NO. 4: Charitable

There are hundreds of organizations that welcome both your money and your time. In addition, most of the charitable organizations in town that are cultivating a female leadership base are vehicles for young people to become involved.

As you pursue involvement and leadership in these circles, don't forget to talk about work.

"Boston is a small town," says Fredi Shonkoff, senior vice president of corporate relations and corporate secretary of Blue Cross Blue Shield of Massachusetts, "and you never know how and when friends, colleagues and acquaintances may be able to support your personal and professional development.

Best of all, you'll meet lots of interesting people to add texture and diversity to your life."

Back in my years at WBZ-TV, colleagues and I from different departments went out after work on Friday nights to catch up on the events of the week. One woman wanted to invoke a rule that we not talk about work. What craziness, I thought. When you go out with your friends, why not find out what's happening at work? Why not hear news from the workplace and why not listen to any advice colleagues can offer? It's important to see work as a part of who you are, an extension of yourself. Conversely, don't monopolize the conversation with just shop talk. Get your antennae up there. You can tell who's burned out and wants only idle chatter, or who wants to engage in office-related grumbling. So, balance your social circle.

The same thing goes for talking about kids on work time and work on kids' time. In the first case, be careful because there is still a sense out there that being a mother can inhibit you from focusing fully on work. As for the second, events that involve kids — Little League, for example — can be a great connector and can spark camaraderie. Just remember not to let the conversation stop there — try to get to know people in the full spectrum of who they are. Your children can be a natural connection in building your relationships, often for the simple fact that many people love kids.

One Spring, my husband and I took our son, John Patrick Thomas, to watch the Red Sox play in Ft. Meyers, FL. With an optimism natural in a 10-year-old, he had brought his baseball glove, hopeful that he'd catch a foul ball. We were seated behind home plate, and midway through the game, Red Sox President and CEO Larry Lucchino stopped by and seemed pleased that John Patrick had brought his glove. "But wait," said Larry, "you're sitting under the net. You won't be able to catch anything." John Patrick shrugged, and I forgot about it. Three innings later, Larry returned with a baseball and dropped it into John Patrick's glove.

On what must have been a busy day for him, he took time out for an act of grace that I won't forget, and neither will John Patrick.

After I had lost my first attempt at running for State Treasurer, I volunteered to chair the Women for John Kerry Senate campaign which gave me the opportunity to meet many women business leaders across the state. As I also knew how important a strong grassroots campaign would be for my next attempt to run for office, I took on the job of leading the effort to collect 10,000 signatures to allow Kerry to get his name on the ballot. Getting to know so many people on this level became invaluable when I ran a second time.

One of my coordinators was adamant that we were going to get more signatures than any other candidate; so she developed an ambitious schedule that had me traveling to dozens of cities and town across the state to personally meet with the grassroots volunteers. When I pointed out that I was holding one particular Saturday open for my upcoming wedding day she said, 'Well, you just will have to reschedule that until after the signature drive is over. I had been dating my fiancé for 9 years. I was 36 years old. She lost that scheduling argument.

Grammar, Presentation and Etiquette –
Creating a Sense of Style

These are simply the tools of the trade. Good grammar does not demand that a woman be able to lecture on the nuances of introductory adverbial phrases, but it does require that she understand the fundamental rules. If you are able to write and speak with confidence in your language, without fear that perhaps you may use a word incorrectly, then you communicate naturally with power and authority.

Some years ago, Kim Harbin was a high-powered marketing director for WBZ-TV in Boston. She was well-spoken and well-acquainted with the English language, including the eight parts of speech. Nevertheless, to give herself that extra edge, she enrolled in a night grammar course at the Harvard Extension School, investing 10 weeks to refine the way she speaks and writes. The investment paid off. She became more articulate, and the new confidence helped her land an even more significant and higher paying job, overseeing all publicity for Disney's ABC Domestic Television in Los Angeles.

The way a person speaks and writes often says more about her than anything on her resume. If you are unsure about your grammar skills, consider a short course at one of the many local universities. Or buy a book and teach yourself. *The Elements of Style* by William Strunk, Jr. and E.B. White is a simple text but considered by many writers to be their bible. *On Writing Well* by William K. Zinsser teaches the art of simple prose and it is certain to improve the way you speak and write. Each book sells for less than $20.

As for presentation, not everyone needs to look like a TV anchor woman, but it does help to have a sense of style. Plenty of off-the-shelf books can help, including Mary Lou Andre's book, *Ready to Wear: An expert's guide to choosing and using your wardrobe*. Try to find your comfort zone, and don't be afraid to ask for help.

When I began working for Channel 4, I didn't have a clothing allowance, but my boss did provide me with a day of counsel by the station's fashion consultant. At my small apartment in Somerville, in my tiny closet, I showed her my three out-of-date jackets. She shuddered, and then she took me to Filene's and helped me pick out tailored clothes. She taught me how to mix and match. It was merely one day, but it was enough to steer me in the right direction. If you don't have access to a personal fashion consultant, seek out the advice of a personal shopper the next time you're in a department store. Be honest about your budget and she will respect it.

While you're there, stop by the make-up counter for application tips. If you're near Boston's Downtown Crossing, I recommend Macy's. If you're in the suburbs, the personal shoppers and makeup consultants are very helpful at Bloomingdale's. Knowing your colors and appropriate styles can go a long way. It won't change who you are, but it will give you confidence.

"Women are still judged by appearances, including by the media, in ways that men are not," said Marylou Sudders, president and CEO of the Massachusetts Society for the Prevention and Cruelty to Children. "It was highly publicized that incoming Speaker of the House Nancy Pelosi appeared at her first press conference in a lilac Armani suit; no one would think to mention what color tie the outgoing Speaker of the House had on that day!"

As for etiquette, many of those pesky rules by Emily Post still ring true — although not all should be followed indiscriminately. Bragging, for example, has often been labeled as an unappealing trait in women, and as a result, many women downplay their successes and keep quiet about accomplishments. Too bad men don't have the same problem. Although bragging can be obnoxious, learning to dance the fine line between boasting and sharing important skills and talents can be important to your career. How else will everyone know how great you are?

You must get across two or three points that show something solid and substantive about you. It's about the manner in which you share it that counts. Whatever you do, don't over talk.

In order to present a polished professional image, you have to be concise, direct, honest, and informed. Shake hands firmly without flexing those muscles you developed lifting barbells at the health club. Look into people's eyes. Dress appropriately. Advocate for number one, and stand up for what you believe in. Shelves of self-help books elaborate on personality pointers.

Another major question of etiquette — when to greet someone with a kiss on the cheek — is tricky. It can be perfectly fine, particularly if you know and feel comfortable with the person. However, in business situations, it's usually better to reserve this enthusiasm for a more informal setting. If you kiss one person, what about the others whom you may not know as well? And if you're being introduced to a large group, do you kiss everyone and leave people with the impression that you once worked at the kissing booth at the state fair back home in Kansas?

One night I was at an event where a friend, who also happened to be a high-ranking public official, was speaking. I had been to his home for parties, and occasionally saw him and his wife socially. In fact, he had recently become a client of my firm. I walked over to say hello and bent down to give him a kiss on the cheek. His discomfort became immediately obvious. "Don't kiss me," he whispered, nervously. "I'm about to give you a state contract!"

Knowing when to brag, when to exude modesty, and when to shake hands instead of planting a firm one on a colleague's cheek are all part of learning the game. The person who never seems to make any mistakes is Bennie Wiley, the former president and CEO of the Partnership, Inc. Bennie is always true to her principles but speaks her mind with grace and understanding. Short of watching Bennie in action, you can find practical etiquette tips in *Emily Post's the Etiquette Advantage in Business: Personal Skills for Professional Success*, written by Peggy and Peter Post.

Poise comes in many guises. Call it personal style. (Think Oprah, Meryl, Condi, Meredith, Anna Wintour, by no means all beauties.) And, contrary though it may sound, developing personal style means not letting anyone tell you what to do. There is no one "right" look. No single "winning" personality.

"Be who you are," says Karen Kaplan. "We are all unique — and there's nothing wrong with playing up what makes us different and being proud of and comfortable with it."

I was at a holiday brunch at a friend's house, and spotted an acquaintance that I hadn't seen for a while. I knew she had had a baby the previous year but she looked pregnant again. So I blurted out 'How are you? I didn't know that you were pregnant again.' And she answered sharply, 'I'm not.' I died right there on the spot. I smiled, said I was sorry and fled into the crowd Lesson learned: think before you speak.

GRACE FEY On: Manners

The Elevator Speech

A wonderful exercise to help develop your own professional voice is perfecting the so-called Elevator Speech. To disciples of business gurus, this is nothing new. But it's worth recapping.

Here's a terrific exposition of the concept and the technique, and it's not just because it comes from my managing director, Diana Pisciotta. "It's one of those great clichés those of us in PR and marketing talk about all the time. But, in real life, when introduced to someone new or when reaching out to a more senior professional in either business or social circles, many of us have downcast eyes and we fumble and mumble awkward phrases.

"When you can't answer the standard 'what do you do' question, then you are missing out on many opportunities," Diana says. You have mere seconds to make an impression, to promote your business, to show that you are a person whom this individual — despite his or her position, experience or existing relationships — will want to know.

Be fully confident in both what you say and how you say it, Diana says. An offhand assessment — "Oh, I'm in PR" — doesn't work. It says nothing about you or your job. And worse, if you deliver the line in a flat tone, your new acquaintance will cast their eyes up to the passing floor numbers and begin counting down to freedom.

For many, it evolves over time into conversation that flows naturally. For example, Diana says: "I work in communications; I'm extraordinarily lucky to be able to help really interesting people think through complicated issues and talk about them in a way that engages the public." Say it with passion, and people will want to know more.

A shortened version that I sometimes use is this: "I'm in PR, half of my clients want me to get them into the news, and the other half want me to keep them out."

In a world where cell phones and BlackBerrys are more captivating than an actual conversation with someone standing in front of you, holding someone's attention can be painfully difficult. But as Dave Yewman, co-founder of Elevator Speech Inc., says: "You never know who's standing next to you at an event — it could be a guy with $4 million burning a hole in his pocket, looking for the next opportunity."

As the man behind www.elevatorspeech.com, and a frequent featured speaking at business conferences across the country, Dave knows the secrets to crafting that illusive 30-second snippet. He says that people go wrong in two areas — they talk only about themselves and fail to mention successful problem-solving or client successes. "People make the mistake of thinking that when people ask what you do, that they actually care," Dave said. "They don't. What they care about is what you can do for them!"

His No.1 tip? Videotape yourself reciting your Elevator Speech. The most common problem may become immediately obvious: it's boring. Dave coaches his clients to think in "inverted pyramids," sharing the most important information first. For example, he once worked with the CEO who was fond of describing his Texas golf company as a multi-channel golf operation. After the third or fourth take, the CEO came up with a more nimble and memorable phrase: "It's like a candy store for golfers."

"You don't have to say everything in 20 seconds, you just have to make it intriguing enough to capture someone's attention — you need an 'aha' moment," Dave said. "A candy store is so compelling because everyone has been in a candy store before.

It also gives you permission from the listener to paint a picture."

Think of your Elevator Speech as a snappy headline, make it sexy and compelling, Dave advises. Tell an anecdote or pick one or two things to focus on. Dave provides this example: A CEO working for a company that makes hand-held devices that played music, videos and movies, described his product as "the next generation PVR." Boring.

"First, 'next generation' just means new, so why not say new? And, second, what's a PVR?" Dave says. "Later the CEO developed the perfect statement: 'It's like a little movie theater in my pocket, or a Tivo to go.'"

Okay, so most executives might pray for frayed cables rather than stuck moments with Elevator Speechmakers. But the concept is a good one, so meet the challenge: Be prepared to sell yourself, fast.

4. Pitch Yourself

A basic skill for young women that doesn't necessarily come naturally, even to the best and the brightest, is how to work a room. No better way to hone and practice your professional voice than at a business-related social event. You hate them you say? You'd rather be home with your (a) lover, (b) dog, (c) kids, (d) dirty laundry, (e) exercise machine, all of the above, or out anywhere else on earth? Well, as Nike says: "Just do it."

I know, I know. It's too much to ask. At the end of a 10-hour work day, you're tired. You want to spend time with your family. You want a private life. Yet, to be a Power Chick, you've got to be out and about the city. You have to be visible, prominent, maybe even a boldface regular.

The benefits of attending events are huge. Don't think merely in terms of charity balls. Many of the 101 run-of-the-mill "in honor of" fundraisers can be key to getting to know more people and enhancing your reputation, your company and your career in the process. There are dozens of smaller dollar fundraisers — political and charitable — as well as breakfasts and socials. Going to these bread and butter events may be the equivalent of working your way up through the farm team. But, if done right, your participation will be noted and rewarded because each event, no matter how minor, has its VIPs, honorees or sponsors in attendance.

You can make the most of the rubber chicken circuit by attending those that have the most potential to draw key players within your field; or, to be blunt, those who can advance your career. Scan trade publications for upcoming events. If you're not a member or not on the invitation list, call and ask about attendance. Most of them welcome anyone who will buy a ticket — and certainly anyone who buys a table, which is a great way for young people to pool resources and get into some of the more selective events.

The Boston Chamber of Commerce can be an invaluable resource. Your company may be a member already, which means reduced ticket prices or the occasional company table. Chamber events cover a broad range of topics — from government affairs to life sciences and the Leading Industries Executives Forums. Don't miss the summer networking event at the Taj (the old Ritz Carlton), the holiday party or the annual dinner. For the holiday event at least, get there early. The chamber usually holds its full board meeting right before the reception. Its biggest names tend to network for the first 30 minutes.

For the more rapidly sold-out or exclusive parties, you may have to call a friend or colleague at a sponsoring company or committee and ask her to secure you a seat. You can also try a pal in the press. They get tons of invites, some of which are "nontransferable," but most of which, sadly, end up in the trash. If she plans to attend, she may be able to bring a guest. That would be you.

Sally Jackson, one of Boston's more colorful Public Relations veterans, used to keep all the invitations that she received, and not because she planned to attend every event. She used the invitations to create a list of who's who in Boston that was comprehensive and meticulously up to date.

If you're looking for invitations, women in public relations are a great source. These are some of the women who know what's happening in the city: Dusty Rhodes, Jan Saragoni, Lynne Kortenhaus, Micho Spring, Colette Phillips, Marlo Fogelman and Helene Solomon.

So scan your invitations or anyone else's, for that matter, for names of the host committees so that you can evaluate who'll be attending. Identify industry events that are likely to draw key players within your field. Get to know what events attract your

clients and referral sources. Then put on your party dress and
go to work.

Arrive on time and use the cocktail portion of the evening to
say hello to friends and colleagues, but also to seek out past
acquaintances and reintroduce yourself. Check out nametags
and recognizable faces. Then, be fearless. Go ahead and introduce yourself to someone you've been dying to meet, or ask a
colleague to make an introduction.

This may provide the opportunity to use that pithy Elevator
Speech, but it's not the time for a full sales pitch.

The Basics of Do and Don't

One of the toughest tasks in skillful partying is getting up the
guts to break the ice. As one young professional put it: "You're
in a room full of powerful people and you know it's great
networking turf, but all you can think is: 'Oh my God, when
can I leave?' I wind up just looking at people's shoes. It's so
much easier."

Coming up with a topic of conversation, especially if you're
feeling intimidated by the firepower in the room, is never easy.
But here are ways to ease the stress.

Find common ground. If you've imbedded yourself alongside
the cheese display and someone comes along that you would
like to chat with, talk about the cheese. Or if you notice someone who looks tan in December, ask if she skis. You know
something about skiing, and off you go.

Ask questions. As one young professional said: "I don't have
much to say in a setting where my professional experience is
limited, so when I meet someone important, and because I
don't have as much to say, I ask questions. I want to know
how'd you get there? How do you do what you do? But

how do you exploit that intellectual curiosity about somebody at that higher level without sounding like a jerk?" You ask and you just keep asking. Trust me: Anyone who has succeeded in the professional world just loves to tell someone else how to navigate it.

Party Spirits

Of course, it's not easy to strut your stuff if you're shaking in your Jimmy Choos. Attending a business-related social event can be unsettling, but remember: Everyone gets intimidated. It's common nature. The best antidote is preparation.

Connect the dots. Before you get there, polish up on who's likely to be attending the event. Then go a step further than merely studying the names, titles and affiliations of people you hope to meet. Do a bit of a search on the online sites of the *Boston Globe*, *Boston Herald*, and the *Boston Business Journal*. For who's who and what's what, check out *Boston Common*, *the Improper Bostonian* or *Stuff@Night*. For an appreciation of the lighter side of Boston, listen to Matty in the Morning on KISS 108FM. Ask a colleague or friend about a special circumstance or noteworthy event in the lives of those who'll be attending. Maybe a son or daughter has been married recently, or perhaps a man has hosted a successful charity ball or a woman's company has made a new discovery. Knowing such information eases the stress at a party and elevates your skill at conversation.

I once met Robert Kraft, before his days as owner of the Patriots. It was an informal courtesy call, but in preparation, I asked a friend at the *Globe* to pull together clips about his business ventures and then I read every article. Mr. Kraft was flabbergasted by how much I knew about him. Years later, I was working as a consultant with the international relief organization CARE, which happened to be looking for a lead sponsor for a large fundraiser. Mr. Kraft had just bought the Patriots and had been in the news — it sparked a connection, so I asked him. Not only did he remember me, but he also agreed to the sponsorship. It's a reminder that preparation pays dividends.

Speaking of the Krafts, Myra Kraft is in the power seat with her husband, sitting shoulder to shoulder. She manages both the Robert and Myra Kraft Family Foundation and the New England Patriots Charitable Foundation, making a powerful impact on the region. She goes even farther with her service on several of the city's most notable boards, including as chair of Combined Jewish Philanthropies, chair of the Boys & Girls Club of Boston from 1996 to 2002, the Boston Foundation, United Way of Massachusetts Bay and Brandeis University.

Now that you know that homework comes first, learn how to read a room when you get there. This applies to business functions like committees and board meetings as well as parties. Figure out who are the power centers, the magnets. Where's the boss? The chairman? The guest of honor? Who are the acolytes? Does anyone seem preoccupied or annoyed? Who's the belle of the ball? Who's been abandoned alone next to the ice sculpture? Who looks awkward and would probably benefit from a big hello from you? Introduce yourself. You'll be remembered.

As for the real spirits, alcohol, limit yourself to one — two if you're a veteran. You'll feel better in the morning.

Maintaining Connections
A pitch-perfect Elevator Speech and spot-on socializing will go for naught if you don't follow up on the connections you've made. You've opened the door, now for heaven's sake, go through it! There are ways to follow up on introductions. They include sending a personal note saying what a pleasure it was to chat and suggesting a future get together, calling to schedule

an appointment, or tendering an invitation to an upcoming event. Emails are okay, but a personal touch is better, especially with older, more traditional VIPs. There are things you can do to make a person remember you. Sending a newspaper article or a link to a website of interest can make a statement.

Sports can be a facile connection. Find out the person's favorite team, follow the statistics, and a few weeks later, send the box scores with a note. Be sure to follow the NCAA college basketball tournament. Many people, even those who don't care a whit about professional sports, follow their college team through March Madness. It's a great icebreaker, albeit short lived. It is important to know that in Boston, conversation is driven by sports and politics. So while you're keeping up with the important stories of the day, know who Hazel Mae is, and don't forget to read the sports page.

Beth Boland, now a partner at Bingham McCutchen, learned the importance of sports when she was a young associate. "My office was right next to another associate who was more blessed with athletic talent than technical legal expertise. Nevertheless, one day one of the partners, who was also athletically inclined, walked into his office and asked if the associate would be interested in attending the symphony with the partner, his wife and some clients," she said. "The light dawned on me that (1) the possibility that this would happen to me was quite slim and (2) it was a lot more effective to be chatting with a client at the symphony than at one's office writing briefs!"

So, let's reinforce the John Spinola rule: Get out of the office.

"Young women should realize they don't get ranking in a firm from billing more hours. They get power and rank from connections," says attorney Andrea Kramer. "One of the ways to distinguish yourself is through whom you know. So take 100 hours off the top. Get out; let people see you're doing something else besides being a billing machine."

Power broker Gloria Larson goes a step further: "Don't be afraid to ask people to go out for breakfast or lunch," she recommends to young women. "I find it inspiring when people ask me for advice. Try to find someone who's doing things that you'd like to see yourself doing someday." (I can only imagine how many will take her up on that. . .better get a new phone line, Gloria).

As you meet new people, be sure to enter the name of each new contact in an electronic file. I recommend an Excel spreadsheet so you can sort by company or interest. Annotate the entry with how and where you met, what he or she does, and any tidbits that might be useful talking points. (For example: She loves dogs, and not just dogs, but spaniels.) Note if you two plan a future meeting. Keep track of birthdays and upcoming weddings. Send a simple card or email. Attend wakes and funerals in support of clients, or send flowers. Acknowledging life's milestones may seem like a simple gesture, but it speaks volumes. People will remember.

I must add that, Gloria Larson's generosity aside, it's usually not a great idea to suggest a social meeting — lunch or drinks, much less dinner — to a new acquaintance who is, to put it plainly, above your station. Save that for someone you struck up a delightful conversation with, but who is also at approximately the same hierarchical level.

And while I'm on the slightly dicey subject of knowing when to make the first move, let's talk about when not to make the last. This is the occasion when that investment banking gal you had a jolly old time chatting with at the Heart Ball, who seemed so interested in having lunch, has now ignored your call or email invitation.

Take the hint. Back off. Take the high ground. The next time you bump into each other, she may well feel chagrined or sufficiently regretful that she really does want to get together — and maybe even do you a good turn.

And if not, neither of you has to have a red face.

Even though it may not always result in a profitable outcome, following up on brief introductions or informal meetings is essential to making and keeping the good contacts that expand your power base and feed your sphere of influence.

To say nothing of good manners.

5. Expand Your Brand

You are your brand. Building and maintaining relationships with sources, mentors and potential clients will expand your network, but there are several other platforms you can use as a jumping off point, including your job and public speaking.

When you go on an interview, look around at the organization, says Carol Goldberg, president of the investment and consulting firm AVCAR Group Ltd. Carol spent 30 years at The Stop & Shop Companies, Inc. She explored the plight of the female executive in *Members of the Club: the Coming of Age of Executive Women*, a book she co-authored with Dawn-Marie Driscoll in 1993.

"Are there women on the senior management team? If not, that's a clue that it will be difficult to advance," Carol says. "That doesn't mean that you shouldn't take the opportunity because it could be a stepping stone. In your interview, ask: What are my opportunities for growth? That will be a signal to them."

Ask yourself:
* Does this job afford me, under the guise of work, the opportunity to meet somebody I don't know?
* Does it allow me to join an organization or help a charity because my manager thinks that's important?
* Does this job allow me to take courses that will improve my skills?

Without changing the job or the title, can my position be more than the job description?

Separation anxiety — fear of leaving the friendly confines of your cubicle or corner suite — attacks all of us, no matter how schooled in public appearances we may be. Here are a few tips on how to cast off the shackles and expand your sphere of influence.

First, see if there are people you want to invite for coffee, just to talk about their personal lives and see how they succeeded in their careers. People are flattered to be asked to talk to people outside of the job. In my business, for example, that may entail looking at clients or reporters and asking, "Who's the reporter that I'd like to get to know just to talk to?" Reporters are very well-connected people and you might learn something. Or, there may be a client that you might want to get to know in a more informal setting. Are there opportunities for you to offer to take them to a civic event or invite them to something that they might enjoy?

Second, make a point to attend two events a month. This will keep you on course and force you to manage your time each week. It's a pro-active approach that prevents you from slipping back into the desk-chair gang and makes building your database a priority.

Third, use the buddy system. Keep your friends and colleagues in the loop about upcoming events, and ask that they return the favor. Attending events with friends automatically expands your number of acquaintances and makes it easier to approach individuals or groups.

Public Speaking

Another key step in your personal outreach program, or marketing yourself, is to hone your public speaking skills and to find opportunities to present at alumni or trade association events. To Vivien Li, executive director of The Boston Harbor Association, public speaking is one of the most important traits of a successful business person.

"Young women benefit from speaking well in public," Vivien says. "Even as an experienced public speaker, I often practice the delivery a number of times before an important speech.

And certainly before a speech that might be emotional, such as when receiving an award or giving a tribute."

Polish your speaking skills by taking a course at a local university. If your firm provides training, sign up for an intensive program — there are dozens to choose from in Boston alone. If you don't have the support of your company, the Boston Center for Adult Education offers affordable, professional programs for about $100 per session.

Lois Phillips, author of *Women Seen and Heard: Lessons Learned from Successful Speakers* said in a web-posted interview with the Center for Women's Leadership at Babson College that "women tend to present themselves as tentative, rather than forceful and confident in delivering their proposals and message. Public speaking is a great way to develop self-confidence that is more global, and the skills transfer beautifully to everyday conversations," she said. "The great thing is that the skills can be learned, once a person is motivated."*

Look for upcoming alumni events at your alma mater. Are there any panels that would benefit from your expertise? Look at trade organizations as well. Identify trends in the industry or timely issues and then approach the organization with a proposal. Remember, speaking engagements are not a time to sell your product or services, but to position yourself as an expert and leader in your field. These will be difficult to come by early in your career, so start small.

For tips on public speaking, check out one of my favorites, Suzanne Bates' book *Speak Like a CEO: Secrets for commanding attention and getting results*. Suzanne provides dozens of helpful hints on the most common mistakes speakers make, and she reveals the secrets of the most successful speakers. You don't have to be a CEO, Suzanne says, to cultivate a powerful voice that is your own.

*Reprinted with permission from the Center for Women's Leadership at Babson College

Invite-only Networking

Public speaking, renewing old acquaintances and maintaining contacts are all keys to expanding your personal brand. Another is to join an informal breakfast or lunch group, which can be particularly valuable because they bring together people from diverse fields. Attendance is often by personal reference, that is, invitation only.

However, many professional women are forming their own groups. Margery Piercey, partner of the CPA and business consulting firm Wolf & Company, for example, selected seven women from different industries for a special monthly breakfast group designed to generate business leads and provide support. Each woman represents a different industry, including public relations, real estate brokerage, architecture, and the construction industry. Each month the group meets for breakfast. Over bagels and coffee they discuss new opportunities, seek advice and expand their circles of connections and business contacts. It's a great resource.

Mentors

Building a relationship with one or more mentors can be helpful to your professional development and also can help build your brand. Mentors, male or female, can provide guidance or candid assessments about issues that you may not want to discuss with your boss. Watch the women you admire in the office — for example, how they respond in uncomfortable situations, the manner in which they present themselves, and their individual leadership style. Learn by observing.

As a young professional in the male dominated engineering field, Liz Levin didn't have many options for a role model, especially since she was always the highest ranking woman in her company. She learned most of her lessons the hard way — by trial and error.

"Now women have so many mentors available that reaching out and getting advice is the best thing that young people can do," says Liz, president of her own management consulting firm, "It saves a lot of angst. I have just started an online advice program to do just that — be available for people in their career so that they don't muck around in the mud and can get to that next step."

In the main, mentoring is a good thing. You can especially benefit if you can find someone in a senior position with whom you can share your questions about self-confidence or other issues that, raised with your supervisor, might leave the impression that you're weak or confused. But you shouldn't be looking for that one special person. Learn to see mentors as an amalgam of people. One person may have a speaking style you admire, another a work ethic. You get the idea. And, if you do find that special one, hold on until it's time to let go.

"The best mentors are those who are willing to challenge you and to provide candid assessments," says Vivien Li, of The Boston Harbor Association.

Meg Vaillancourt, senior vice president of corporate relations and executive director of the Red Sox Foundation, prefers to think of mentoring as a two-way conversation. She says that individuals can understand how to collaborate much more effectively if they learn from each other.

"A number of organizations do a great job of cultivating future leaders, but there might be room for a more targeted effort, where four or five people from different organizations, mid-career, work together on a common challenge our community faces," she said. "In my job, I deal with nonprofits every day. Sometimes they are looking not only for financial support, but also for ideas on how their organization can improve their outreach. And I've found that they also always have something to teach me...Another benefit of having a two way conversation is that it keeps you young. Forget the BOTOX® — have a two-way conversation instead."

And who says it has to be woman to woman? The consensus of our focus group was that having a mentor was desirable, in fact, expected. But only about half the 20 or so young professionals were satisfied that they'd found one, and of those, most said the mentor was a man. Indeed, a recent study of more than 200 Fortune 500 leaders found that almost all of the small number of women bosses — 23 — had cultivated a powerful male mentor.

Among my first mentors was John Sasso, who was chief of staff under Gov. Michael Dukakis in the 1980s and later became known in Boston as "the master strategist." Sasso was able to step outside the day-to-day work for the Governor to listen to me when I considered leaving my job as a press secretary at the State House. It was a gut wrenching decision as I worried about appearing disloyal. "Your heart seems really into making the change," John told me. In the ensuing years, he has continued to be a great sounding board for professional questions. By the way, when I decided to make the move, I was afraid to tell then Gov. Dukakis. So I talked to Mrs. Dukakis, who was fortifying. She smiled and said: "Oh, go for it."

Another friend from my days in state government is Paul Levy, president and CEO of Beth Israel Deaconess Medical Center. I recently called upon him for advice on a matter related to managing personnel in my company. His advice helped me at a difficult juncture. In my work today, I don't have a "boss" but I still need mentors.

Risk and Reward
Attracting attention through outreach is a win-win set-up. But sometimes you have to be your own audience, even if that

We all look at others who we admire and try to emulate them. For several years, I had the privilege of working for Wayne Budd, an amazing leader. I was exposed to his unique leadership style on a daily basis. In staff meetings, he would gather his direct reports at a round table and say: 'Now here's the business challenge, folks, and I need your assistance. I need the benefit of getting advice from each of you.' What always impressed me was that he so strategically brought out the considerable diversity of thought amongst us, enabling him to hear a vast range of options. This allowed him to make the best business decisions. His thoughtful, collaborative and confident style demonstrates true leadership.

means being your own heckler. You know what I mean. That voice within you says: "You're slouching in your chair." Or, "Stand straight." Or, "C'mon, take a few risks."

It happened to me in 1993, toward the end of eight years as editorial director at WBZ-TV. It was clear the station was reducing its coverage of politics and public affairs. I don't think I stayed too long there, but it was hard for me to begin casting about for my next opportunity. One day I had the good fortune to meet Pamela McDermott, one of Boston's original Power Chicks. Pam had started her own public relations firm. Over lunch, she suggested that journalism would be a good foundation for a career in communications consulting. She persuaded me to join her firm, McDermott/ O'Neill, a move that made it possible a few years later to start my own business.

Fear of financial risk, never mind public failure, may become a consideration when a woman achieves a modicum of success. She can be hobbled by the fact that she's afraid of losing what she has.

ELLYN MCCOLGAN
On: Taking Risks
Ellyn McColgan, long considered one of the most likely candidates to eventually assume the helm of Fidelity's top position, recently resigned. A powerful and thoughtful woman, she will no doubt emerge again as a powerhouse in business.

If you're going to be big and brave and bold, you're going to take risks. It's only natural that every now and then you'll come up short on something. Throughout my career, I've been asked to do several turn around jobs, jobs that had big challenges but also could have big wins at the end. It wouldn't surprise you to know that I suppose there were some failures along the way. When I look back on those things they were probably some of my biggest learning experiences. The good news is that now I know what works and what doesn't work and I can smell it in the air.... So failure, while it may be humbling, is in fact one of the most important and best teachers you'll ever have.*

*Reprinted with permission by the Commonwealth Institute

Believe me, I'm not cavalier — change is difficult. In your 20s you have margin for error. (Think the office holiday party.) In your 30s, you are taken more seriously, and it's the decade to consolidate your professional talents. But it's a time, too, when you may become restless at your job, and yet find yourself reluctant to change because you have others, family or employees, who are dependent on you.

It's traumatic to take that personal, professional and financial risk, to start a business or to go back to school. And, to be honest, it gets harder as you get older because the options are fewer and the risk greater. So don't listen to what your best girlfriend or your uncle says. Put yourself in a quiet place, weigh the options and follow your heart and your passion.

6. Power Chicks in Training:
Dos and Don'ts

As you expand your leadership role, both at work and in the community, mistakes will occur. Even the most polished professional woman has a "most embarrassing moment" or two in her closet — some of us have many. We'll all make social gaffes along the way.

In fact, many of Boston's Power Chick's admit that they still occur, as former Delta Dental of Massachusetts President and CEO Kathy O'Loughlin confesses: "I lectured once for an hour with my fly open and my white shirt sticking out. My slip fell down once when I was up on stage accepting an award — that was hilarious. Social mistakes are what they are — there is humor in it because we all make them. They can be the funniest moments of our lives, especially if we can laugh at ourselves and permit others to do the same. It's really important, however, not to make the same mistake twice — social errors can be perceived as incompetence by some."

While we couldn't possibly list all the barriers you may encounter throughout your career, we'll start with some basic dos and don'ts that are important for Power Chicks-in-Training.

Take a compliment with grace.
It sounds simple, even obvious, but how many times have you, or someone you work with, brushed off praise? If you are embarrassed by approbation, then the person who gives you the compliment will feel uncomfortable. Taking credit for your hard work is not bragging, nor is it inappropriate. If "thank you" seems inadequate, then respond instead with: "I learned a lot on that project." Or, "It was a team effort." Or, "It was difficult, but I'm glad that it worked out." The person bestowing the compliment, in many cases senior managers or even your boss, wants you to be proud of your accomplishments. If your good work redounds well for your boss and makes her proud, then why shouldn't you be proud, too?

Don't cozy up just to men.

The men, historically, may be powerful, but do not underestimate the senior women at the table. If you give them the cold
shoulder, they will notice, it will bug them and they will
remember. When a young woman immediately targets the guys
in the office, it's obvious, obsequious and offensive, particularly
to women but also to some men. That's not you. Don't fall into
the trap.

Always tell the truth.

Gloria Larson, now president of Bentley College and former
U.S. deputy director of consumer protection under President
George H.W. Bush, to this day remembers her first experience
with what she calls "real-time candor." She was preparing a key
government document for the U.S. Congress. After it had
been printed and bound and was ready for distribution, Gloria
realized that she had made what she calls a huge mistake. "I
had to tell my boss first thing in the morning," she recalls, and it
wasn't pretty. "Facing up to your mistakes is a good lesson. Tell
the truth at the time the issue arises. It's not good enough to
look back on a situation and tell the truth retrospectively."

Don't' let your mistakes consume you.

As Carol Fulp says, it's unproductive. "Just recently I have
begun to think of myself as successful. And success is not about
money, power or visibility; it's about being at peace with
oneself. We all work hard, and we all are hard on ourselves.
And if we don't do something right, we get knots in our stom-
ach from the stress we put on ourselves. After all these years, I
finally feel comfortable with who I am, and so now, when I
make a mistake, it's just a mistake. That one act doesn't define
the person I am."

Do not underestimate lessons learned on the playing field

I came to this realization later in life. As a young activist in the
early 80s, I used to say: "Spare me from men who think that

Don't cry as a professional woman.

Just don't.

**GLORIA
LARSON
On: Crying**

sports are a metaphor for life." Well, I'm a little older now, and guess what? The metaphors sometimes work. Admittedly, there's a world of difference between my generation and the women today in their 20s (thanks to Title IX). Watching my son on the baseball field, I can see how sports translate into business. For example, you don't have to like someone to be a supportive teammate. That's a reminder we could all use at some point in our careers.

**VIVIEN LI
On: Reputation**

Most of us will work 30 years or more – we all need to remember that work colleagues and professional acquaintances will often remember you for a long time after you move on in your career. I can't tell you the number of times that I have heard people say, "I worked with so-and-so and she was "blank." Your reputation follows you, and you want to be remembered as the colleague who was hard working and a good employee, as opposed to the one who got drunk at the firm's annual Christmas party, or who did the minimum amount of work necessary to get by, or was careless.

During my first campaign for the State Senate in 1990, a well-respected political reporter for the largest regional paper asked me in my first meeting with him if I was married. ("No.") Then, his follow-up was, "Do you have a boyfriend?" ("Yes.") I was blown away by the next question: "Is it serious?" ("Did my mother put you up to this?") I tried to make a joke, but it really struck me that there was no way he would have asked that line of questioning to a man. It was the beginning of my understanding that gender shades many professional careers. You can either accept that and figure out how to use it to your advantage when possible, and overcome it when it isn't a plus, or you can change your career direction and fight bias. I choose the first course, but admire (and am grateful to) those who choose the latter.

Make Words Count
Don't be a silent movie. Know when to listen, but know when to speak, too.

My particular nightmare on this score occurred within the first week or two at my job at WBZ-TV, Channel 4. The station was hosting a role-playing workshop to help us work more as a team, and I was asked to sit on the panel. Well, having just started the job, I didn't quite know what to do or what to say.

I ended up sitting on the panel for a whole morning and did not say a word the entire time, not a single word, and why? It grieves me to admit it now, but I was embarrassed that if I said something, it would be wrong.

I had ignored a lesson hammered home in high school — do your homework! I didn't know what the workshop entailed. I didn't know what was expected. Even if I didn't say much, I should have said something. I was back in high school again, and having neglected to do my Latin homework, the teacher called on me, and I was humiliated. I found out later that people were joking about whether I was mute — it's a memory that still haunts me.

On the other hand, there's a downside to speaking up at the wrong time. Once the idea is on the table, it isn't necessarily yours anymore. Remember the FedEx ad where the low-key kid's idea is co-opted by the CEO?

Joyce Murphy, vice chancellor and chief operating officer of UMass Medical School/ Commonwealth Medicine, recalls a real-life echo. "I was in a middle management position at a meeting of 25-30 people. The CEO asked for input on a particular subject, and I volunteered a course of action, but was not acknowledged. Within seconds, almost interrupting me, the man two seats down from me offered in a very loud voice the very same suggestion. He was greeted by very positive comments from the CEO and other leaders. I should note that I was one of two women in the room and the other one was taking the minutes."

How many times have women experienced a similar situation? Carol Goldberg, the former Stop & Shop executive, said it still happens to her. "I've been in a meeting, said something and nothing happens, yet a man will then say the same thing later and suddenly everyone thinks it's a great idea," she says. "You can't be rude, but you also can't let it go. I say 'Oh Max, I'm so glad you expressed what I said; only you said it better.'"

If you take Carol's advice and keep the twinkle in your eye, the whole room will get the point.

Hone your communications skills to be your most persuasive. It makes you memorable. No boors or bores allowed. But don't gush. At the same time, here's the most important word of advice. It's as vital as it is simple. It's a single word.

Listen.

In my focus group on the characteristics essential to a Power Chick, no attribute was mentioned more often than the art of listening well.

A woman in the Foreign Service, accustomed to going to different countries, meeting new people, and putting herself in new situations, told me years ago that listening is one of the most important skills in the business world. Listening well involves hearing what people say and also interpreting their body language. Look attentive. Always remember that they will be observing the same aspects in you.

"There is no better way to make a good, and lasting, impression than being able to repeat things in a way that shows you've really heard what the person said," one woman said. "I can't say enough how listening has helped me in my life."

Business Lunch Behavior
If you're hosting a business lunch, you select the time and place. Know the maitre d' so he can call you by name and call ahead to learn his name so that you don't have to squint at his name badge as you welcome your guests. Familiarize yourself with the menu by looking at the restaurant's website. Give your credit

card in advance or otherwise arrange for payment. Check the bill, but don't quibble over pennies.

To put everyone at ease (and if the budget can stand it), recommend one or more of the expensive items on the menu. Then, don't order a hot dog and water for yourself. If a guest is running late, wait 15 minutes, and then suggest that your other guests order. If it's just two of you, and she fails to show after half an hour, leave without feeling guilty. Cell phones have made the likelihood of such emergency exits rare these days.

If you're the guest, don't over-order. Acting as though you never get out to eat — never mind wasting your host's money — is uncouth. Allow the host to signal when the meal/meeting is over. If she wants to linger, so do you. When you're finished, thank the host; praise the restaurant, the food and the service. And please, even if you have a cute puppy, no doggy bags.

One of my worst business/social gaffes happened a long time ago, but it is still mortifyingly fresh. I was just out of college, and new to Boston from the Midwest. This is not to say I was ill-mannered, of course, but I did not know Boston well. One day, a high-level woman in the State House office where I worked took me to breakfast at the Ritz Café. Well, breakfast at the Ritz in those days, the mid-80s, was the ultimate power place. I think she took me there because she wanted to help me meet important people, to become comfortable in that environment, and to understand that the Ritz-Carlton was the place for a power breakfast.

We sat at a window seat looking out to Newbury Street, and we had a lovely breakfast. Now, I'd been to restaurants many times, but I had never seen these cute little individual jelly jars that were on the table between us. I thought my boyfriend would think they were darling, and so I took them. She didn't say anything, but she must have looked at me and thought: Who is this woman? I take her to the Ritz and she pockets the jelly jars?

7. Get Involved

So, now you're ready to put your talents to work. A satisfying way to get your feet wet in the currents of good causes, especially if you're not a natural "joiner," or if you eschew the politics that exist even in the most altruistic groups, is to pick a backyard issue that might overlap with your interests. Inquire at your local YMCA or find out if your local neighborhood development corporation needs help. You could also help with planting gardens — from the Back Bay to the burbs.

You are likely part of the generation that participated in community service work in high school or college. As an adult, such service can be vastly more satisfying because you have even more to offer. Fundraising, philanthropy and volunteerism are seen as corporate, civic and caring. And, to be sure, they provide an indirect way to get people of power to know you and your skills.

Courtney Forrester, director of special events for the Isabella Stewart Gardner Museum and one of the city's most visible young fundraisers, notes that she initially chose charities compatible with where she lives, which is a stone's throw from the Public Garden. Courtney became a member of the nonprofit Friends of the Public Garden. Then, when she adopted her now 6-year-old beagle Max, she helped the Mass. Society for the Prevention of Cruelty to Animals, which runs the venerable Angell Memorial Animal Hospital in Jamaica Plain. Perhaps even closer to home, Courtney says she began supporting the Massachusetts General Hospital's Children Storybook Ball after her daughter was treated at MGH.

"It won't stick if it's not a personal connection," Courtney says. "After all, it's your personal time. If I'm going to give up bath time with my one-year-old daughter, it better be for something that I feel strongly about."

Your company may also encourage community involvement.

Each year Michael E. Mooney, managing partner of the Boston law firm Nutter McClennen & Fish, gives a pep talk to new young associates nervous about fitting in and succeeding at a large downtown firm. He always provides a great nugget to the incoming class: "I have the absolute 100 percent key to your success," he says. Ears perk up: What is it? What do we need to do?

His advice, in a word: Volunteer. "If somebody needs something done, whether it's at work or someone who needs someone on their team, raise your hand. You need somebody on the committee for this year's events? I can do that. Show that you are a can-do kind of person."

When you volunteer, don't just go to meetings. Be prepared to commit. Figure out what leadership opportunities are available. Get on a committee. Do the job right, and you could become a candidate for the executive board. Carol Goldberg's book, Members of the Club, calls connections in the broader business and civic community "personal currency." Their value cannot be overestimated.

A second strategy for becoming involved is to leverage company support. First, research the organization in which you are interested. Present a proposal to your manager, and ask if there is anyone else in the company to whom you can talk about joining. Whether a presence at a charity or civic event is the solo you or an entire table, the exposure among corporate leaders and community benefactors (not to mention the press) accrues good will for your firm as well as you. Ask your managers if there is, or can be, money set aside for corporate donations.

Once you have the support of your company, figure out exactly what you could do for the new organization. Ask the executive director out for coffee. Explain that you can help sell tickets to the next big event, or that you can decorate or sell ads for a program book — anything in lieu of writing a check. Remember, nonprofits value "sweat equity."

"You can't wait for someone to ask you — you have to call people, send a note or write directly to the President saying: I want to volunteer," said Kathy Taylor, associate vice president for new market development for Elderhostel. "Most of the time if you send a note to the president he or she will pass it along to his subordinate; any subordinate will pay attention to a note that the president passes along."

Don't forget Beacon Hill — after all, you don't have to be a professional lobbyist to become involved in issues close to your heart. Take a lesson from The Public Policy Institute's Executive Director Judy Meredith. She was a housewife with five children, two of whom were adopted, when, as a member of an adoptive parent group, she learned that a Massachusetts law that prohibited many families from adopting a child from a mother of a different religion. Working together, Judy's group eventually found that, due to the law, nearly 2,000 children were stuck in foster care.

"I remember raising my hand to volunteer to chair the new legislative committee and got lucky on three counts. My own state representative was willing to help us meet with the religious community and draft legislation acceptable to them. He briefed me on the how-a-bill-becomes-law process and schedule, and advised me on what needed to be done and when over the course of the year," she says in her *Real Clout Workbook*, a guide to grassroots lobbying. "Secondly, armed with my group's membership list and a phone, I was able to organize an enthusiastic network of folks who would talk to their own legislators in the district. Finally, the organization raised money to pay for phones, postage and child care so that some of us could set up a communications network and spend some time at the State House."

After a whirlwind of meetings with state legislators and families on Beacon Hill and across Massachusetts, Judy and her group prevailed. Judy is one of the most well respected and influential lobbyists on issues of economic justice, and is a dramatic example of how you can channel your passion and interests to achieve powerful changes.

Closing the Gap

In an effort to reignite civic compassion and commitment among young professionals and close the "leadership gap," several of Boston's nonprofits are seeking younger board members who not only make corporate and small personal donations, but also plan large fundraisers and service events. Collectively, they are capturing a new voice in Boston and bringing a new generation to action. In fact, they are becoming a larger part of nonprofit fundraising as their creativity, energy and passion fuel successful new ways to attract young energy into older institutions.

Special Notes:
There are many women who go above and beyond in service to the community and in their commitment to helping women at all stages of professional development. There are so many that I could not possibly name them all. Here are a few whose names stand out, and whom I have had the pleasure of knowing personally: **Joyce Plotkin**, president of the Massachusetts Technology Leadership Council; **Marianne Ajemian**, a partner at Nutter McClennen & Fish and president of Commercial Real Estate Women; **Lois Silverman**, founder and chair of The Commonwealth Institute and chair of Beth Israel Deaconess Medical Center's Board of Trustees; **Barbara Lee**, principal of the Barbara Lee Family Foundation; **Linda Whitlock**, president and CEO of the Boys & Girls Club of Boston; **Catherine D'Amato**, president and CEO of the Greater Boston Food Bank; **Deborah Jackson**, CEO of the American Red Cross of Massachusetts Bay; **Joanne Hilferty**, president and CEO of Morgan Memorial Goodwill Industries; **Patricia Foley**, president of Save the Harbor/Save the Bay; **Joan Wallace-Benjamin**, president and CEO of the Home for Little Wanderers; and **Marian Heard**, former president and CEO of United Way of Massachusetts Bay and founding president and CEO of the Points of Light Foundation, a national volunteer network. Their passion for civic engagement, not to mention hard work, launched them into the upper echelons of Boston's most venerable organizations. These women have done an extraordinary amount for young women in the city. If you find yourself in their presence, genuflect.

Organizations like the Massachusetts Society for the Prevention of Cruelty to Children (MSPCC), United Way and the Friends of the Public Garden are cultivating high-profile groups that are making an impact on the bottom line. The Institute of Contemporary Art, under the direction of Jill Medvedow, has also made great strides in tapping into young leaders.

The MSPCC's Young Professionals Board, which includes members between the mid-20s to early 40s, raises thousands each year for the MSPCC's Kid's Day After School Program. The Young Friends of the Public Garden's Green and White Ball, one of the biggest ticket items under the young professional events at $1,000 per ticket, raises a sizeable share for the Boston Public Garden, Boston Common and Commonwealth Avenue Mall.

Many of these young professional groups are only a few years old and are still growing, and so, it's an ideal time to become involved. As interest grows, so do opportunities. Several groups are branching off into subcommittees to accommodate interest and to maximize involvement. Some, like the United Way's young professional board, provide different options: one committee plans volunteer projects, a second raises awareness of United Way through a series of networking and social events, and a third developments events to cultivate leadership skills among its members.

Combined Jewish Philanthropies offers opportunities for young professional leadership and involvement, including a young leadership division. Its various industry networking groups are also open to young professionals, including financial services, healthcare, real estate, and technology. The Jewish Community Relations Council of Greater Boston, led by one of the state's most effective leaders, Nancy Kaufman, is also committed to developing leaders and promoting volunteerism.

Don't feel ready yet for one of these "training boards?" There are several leadership programs in Boston that prepare early and mid-career professionals for that next step. The Boston Chamber organizes Boston's Future Leaders, The Boston

CAROL FULP
On: Community

You can't be a leader in your business unless you are a leader in your community. My Aunt Gertrude was a huge icon in her community in the Virgin Islands. When she died, my cousins and I realized there would never again be anyone in our lives like her. We knew it was our responsibility to each take a part of her and carry on, and in that way her legacy would continue. Everything I do in the community is because Aunt Gertrude lived – whether it was founding Great Encounters for Girls to provide camp scholarships, creating Boston Women Build in the Bayou, or ensuring that 200 of our city kids have summer jobs. I would never have had the passion or courage to do this work without Aunt Gertrude. She continues to be with me every day. In fact, I have one of her favorite sayings framed on my desk: 'When it is time to be the hammer, strike; when it is time to be the anvil, bear it.' This always inspires me and gives me strength, and I hope, humility.

Center for Community and Justice (LeadBoston) provides additional programs and the Emerging Leaders Program at UMass Boston offers a high-profile program for mid to senior level business professionals. The Partnership, Inc., led by Beverly Edgehill, also provides training for professionals of color at every stage of their career. Perhaps you are eligible to participate. Often it takes the support of your company and someone to nominate you.

The Center for Women & Enterprise is also a great resource for any woman who has thought about starting her own business. The center provides training courses at both ends of the spectrum — from exploring to launching and fostering a new company.

Getting Started

So let's review the basics about community service and becoming a good candidate for the nonprofit board of directors or the young professionals board of your favorite organization. We know that a six figure gift to a charitable organization will get the attention of the nominating committee, but short of that type of largesse, be a giver of you time instead. Here are a few steps that will steer you in the right direction.

1. RESEARCH

First ask yourself what are the causes about which you are passionate? If you would like to serve on the board of a non-profit, find out about the person who leads the organization. The executive director often recommends people to the nominating committee of the board — a key group to know. However, any board member could be your "godmother." Check out the list of members to see if you or if someone you know might be able to make an introduction. Remember, the Boston Club has a committee devoted to helping women secure board seats. Considering the fact that the Boston Club includes more than 800 members, if you ask enough people, someone will know one. Ask the member to clue you in on the organizations that are looking for board members and reach out. If you have the resources, you may want to consider joining the Boston Club, it's a great resource for professional women.

2. VOLUNTEER

Many organizations have committees that are open to non board members, usually fundraising in nature. Ask how you can join one. Most nonprofits welcome the help of volunteers in their programs. If you get involved in this way, reach out to the executive director and board chair. Let them know about your experience, and offer observations.

3. YOUR HAT IS IN THE RING – MAKE THE MOST OF IT.

So you've gotten to know the executive director. You've passed muster with the nominating committee. Yes! You've been elected to the board. Board leaders prefer to share the table with members who are energetic and willing to give time, talent and treasure. So jump right in and join a committee. Many board members typically wait a year before choosing a committee. That's a mistake. Start making a difference and build your nonprofit resume now.

4. NEXT STEP

You have worked on a subcommittee for a year or two and are ready for the next step – chairing the next event, or maybe the finance group. The committee leadership positions are often a ticket to the coveted executive board – the group that drives the direction and agenda of the entire organization. It's an important stepping stone.

5. A WORD OF CAUTION

You've done everything right, but it doesn't feel right. That is to say, you've made it on the board, but your comments are lost in the discussion and you're not going to be asked to chair a committee. Perhaps the organization is run by "insiders" or "the old boys network." It's time to channel your energies in a new direction.

One of my favorite board chairmen is Stephen Karp, who presides over Children's Hospital Boston's Board of Trustees. Steve, who is also chair and CEO of New England Development, is ranked in Forbes' list of the 400 Richest Americans in 2006. It's important to become involved in a board where your voice can be heard, he once told me. If the time comes that you feel your time will be better spent elsewhere, resign with grace. Cite the pressure of other commitments or wait until your term expires.

On the way to the top
The boards of Boston's hospitals, universities and cultural institutions are in a stratosphere of their own, mainly due to the fact that they hold fiduciary responsibility and represent the most committed devotees of the organization. Board members are typically grateful patients, alumni or patrons. Read: Wealthy or incredibly successful (or both). If they are not high net worth, they are probably providing an expertise or personal experience that is relevant, or possess a level of highly coveted professional expertise. Don't despair just yet. There is a way in the door.

Many of these institutional nonprofits also have a board of visitors or overseers. Members of these groups serve as ambassadors of the organization, and it's often from this group that the board members are chosen. Therefore, consider it an honor to be asked to serve. Take the leap. Make the most of the experience. Just don't forget to tell the chair about your long-term goal.

Corporate Boards
In business, a corporate board position alone equals power. Unfortunately, the men are keeping most of those seats warm. In the boardrooms of corporations across the state, women are grossly underrepresented.

In fact, women directors make up just 9.9 percent of the corporate boards of the Massachusetts' 100 largest public companies — 45 of which don't have any women represented at all, according to a 2005 study by Bentley, Mercer and The Boston Club.

"There is a business issue here," says Patricia Flynn, Bentley trustee professor of economics and management and co-author of the report. "Strong financial performance and good corporate governance are positively correlated with the presence of women directors. Yet, progress is so slow, if we didn't report the findings with one decimal place, you'd miss it!"

The issue has raised more than a few eyebrows and several organizations are taking the lead to make sure the numbers spike, rather than crawl, in the near future. The Boston Club for one, has made a big commitment to change the status quo.

Nancy Leaming, an executive who not only chairs the American Red Cross of Massachusetts Bay, but also sits on several corporate boards had this to say about obtaining a seat at the table: "Despite the fact that more search firms are now recruiting for board seats, most (excluding Fortune 500) are found as a result of a personal connection. Become involved in the Boston Chamber or UMass young leaders programs, or join a business group or nonprofit board.

What do corporate boards look for? The list is long but includes:
- Specific expertise — financial, marketing
- Certain personality traits: articulate, supportive, self-confident
- Demographics are sometimes relevant
- And, very importantly, someone who will be a good cultural fit with the rest of the board.

The Eternal Juggle

Finding the proper balance between work and a private life can sometimes seem like an urban myth. It's easy to let work consume your life, particularly when you're taking the extra steps to network and build your list of contacts. As many young professional women know, you don't have to have kids to find yourself juggling too many obligations.

Angela Neal, an associate at Bingham McCutchen, found that long hours at the office were difficult to balance with the need to be with family and friends, even more so when she tried to squeeze into her schedule the time needed for one of her favorite passions, jogging. Despite the onerous schedule, she manages, and her secret? Being spontaneous and flexible.

"If you've been putting in long days at work and suddenly find yourself without anything that needs to be done right away, leave at 3 or 4 PM and do whatever it is that you've been missing," she says. "Extend your vacation by an extra day if your presence at work isn't immediately needed. And be willing to make sacrifices for things that are important to keep your life balanced — squeeze in that run, no matter how long the workday. Taking advantage of the windows between overwhelming workloads, or making windows even when there doesn't seem to be time for anything but working and sleeping, can recharge your battery and make you a happier, healthier, and more productive person overall."

So what happens when you add kids into the mix? Wendy Sachs, a former Capitol Hill press secretary and award-winning producer for Dateline NBC, asked that question when she had her first child. In her book, *How She Really Does It: Secrets of the Successful Stay-at-Work Moms*, Wendy provides tips based on 200 interviews with working mothers.

"You have to have excellent child care. You have to believe that when your children aren't with you that they're in really good hands. The crunch time I think is really zero to five, or zero to six years old, when the kids really aren't in school yet and there's no place to really send them and their days aren't occupied by school," she said in a 2005 interview with the Milwaukee Journal Sentinel. "...The other piece of it is having a spouse who's really helpful in helping out with the child care, with the household responsibilities, with making dinner, with doing laundry. It shouldn't all fall on the mother's shoulders. The third element of it is having flexibility within your job, whether that's working four days a week, or three days a week or telecommuting. Having some control over your own schedule was really important. That made it all work."

Wendy also pointed out that women who wait to have children may also have an easier time juggling work and motherhood.

"One of the benefits...is that they really establish themselves and employers don't want to lose them. More and more employers are realizing how valuable these women are, and they are making accommodations," she said.*

If work/life balance is important to you, make sure you ask the right questions before you accept a job. Look at the women in management positions — do they have families? Do they work at home one or two days a week? Can they take a few hours off if they need to take their child to the doctor? Corporate culture is important.

The good news is that the rules are changing. Even law firms, long notorious for the 80-hour work weeks for those in the partner track, have relaxed. More women are becoming partners, without having to surrender their personal life, especially their children. This is not a matter of gender. Family matters — to women and to men.

One of the biggest changes from when I was younger is that men want to be active parents, they see child-rearing as a partnership. But if a woman thinks she can have a bunch of kids and continue to work 12-hour days, she ought to have her head examined.

First and foremost, know your limits. A life of multi-tasking and a whirlwind of business and networking events is not for everyone. If you are limited in how much time you can take from family in the evening, then carefully choose the events you attend, and limit the number. When work begins to take over, all of us have to set boundaries — figure out your limits and how to deal with encroachments. For example, you might earmark Sunday as family day, which means no emails, no business calls, no BlackBerry. Or, if you drive your child to school each morning, turn off the phone and focus on your child.

Make dates with your friends, spouse or children and make sure you keep them. Working into the night consistently creates isolation and unhappiness.

"You can't be afraid to ask for help," said Allison O'Neil, an attorney with Craig and Macauley. "Female professionals should not be afraid to go to Whole Foods on the way to a dinner party. The days when women would work a full day and go home and bake a pie before dinner are over. You've also got to have a partner who supports the decisions you make. Without kids, there are times you hate your job — it's not kids who make you hate your job."

Twenty years ago, a *Boston Business Magazine* report found that more than half of the hundreds of female executives

We both had jobs that we loved, but over time we found that we were all too often trying to force our son into situations that worked for us and the nanny but not for him. It was my husband who came to recognize that it wasn't right. He said: 'You have a fabulous career and a corporate salary.' So he became a stay-at-home dad. My a-ha moment was that I could never do the job the way it needed to be done, not just my day job, but all of the evening activities which present special challenges for a woman at a certain level of her career. I could not do any of it without the support of my husband as a full-time parent.

JOANNE JAXTIMER
On: Family
Joanne Jaxtimer, senior vice president and director of corporate affairs for Mellon New England's Boston office, adopted at age 42. She felt it was helpful to her career to gain solid experience before starting a family.

surveyed did not have children, and nearly half of those said it was by choice. Today, say our young professionals, the executive suites seem more welcoming to mommies. Essentially, though, balance is attainable only if you can buy it, and even then, perhaps not.

"There will be times when you want to give up because it's hard for us to juggle — the world asks very much of women, and now we're asking to get involved in charity and civic events too," said Patricia McGovern, general counsel of Beth Israel Deaconess Medical Center, a former member of the Massachusetts State Senate and a former gubernatorial candidate. "We have come a great distance and made tremendous strides by learning this 'juggling' skill. Look at Nancy Pelosi and Therese Murray. There are so many who have succeeded and serve as role models for us all."

Final Words

You're a young woman in the workforce and that makes you essential to the task of making Boston an even better city. The ever optimistic Gloria Larson has said: "As women in business, we aren't where we used to be, but we're not yet where we are going to be."

In this enlightened cradle of democracy that gave birth to the American Revolution and countless other social movements along the way, the emergence into leadership positions of highly educated, socially active and involved women has been a slow progression. And while it's worth celebrating our successes, there are miles to go.

So, think of this guidebook, in a small way, as a call to action.

If the collective wisdom of the women I've met along the way were distilled, the elixir would contain the following ingredients:

1. PASSION

Be passionate about your choices both in your career and the causes to which you devote your time outside of work. Passion will sustain you on the days when work seems overwhelming and self confidence is in low supply. "Being passionate, tenacious and assuming leadership opportunities will position a young woman to be recognized and rewarded," says Sandra Fenwick of Children's Hospital Boston. "Finding work that is not work but rather a challenging and fulfilling experience and blending that with a balanced personal, social and spiritual life is my key to enduring success."

2. FLEXIBILITY

Once you've made choices, be ready to be flexible. Women have waited for centuries for a seat in the executive office and change does not come overnight, especially when it involves the relinquishing of power. Don't be discouraged. Make course corrections when necessary.

3. ENGAGEMENT

The willingness, the desire, the need to be a part of the important events of your day and in your community will take you a long way. A commitment to more than work. A commitment to more than home. Engage your life with the lives of others in an affirmative, proactive and disciplined way.

And if you do all this — if you combine drive and hard work, if you take the time to expand your contacts and clout, and if you're active in professional groups and involved in causes, then people will respect you, value what you think and appreciate what you do.

And, guess what?

You're a Power Chick.

Appendices

Annual "Must Attend" Events

Date		Price
January	Big Brothers: The Big Night	$$$
January	Boston Chamber of Commerce: Pinnacle Awards	free
January/February		
	WGBH: Food & Wine Auction	$$
February	Cam Neely Foundation:	
	Betting on a Cause & a Cure	$$$$
February/March		
	Boston Municipal Research Bureau Annual Meeting	$
February/March		
	Massachusetts Taxpayers Foundation Annual Meeting	by invite
March	The Joey Fund and the Cystic Fibrosis Fund –	
	Kevin Corner Pocket Celebrity Billards Tournament	$$$$
March	Massachusetts Horticultural Society:	
	New England Spring Flower Show Preview	$
Spring	Crittenton Women's Union:	
	Amelia Earhart Award Luncheon	$$
April	Opening Day at Fenway Park	$–$$$
April	Boston Marathon	free
April	Citizens Schools: A WOW! Affair	$$
April	Urban Improv: Banned in Boston	$
April	Share Our Strength: Taste of the Nation	$$
April	Boston Public Library: Literary Lights Annual Dinner	$$–$$$$
April	Red Cross of Massachusetts Bay:	
	Clara Barton Awards Dinner	$$$
April	MSPCC: Together Against Abuse	$$
May	Health Care for All Annual Gala	$$
May	Insitute of Contemporary Art: Sapphire Necklace Gala	$$$$
May	American Heart Association: Boston Heart Ball	$$$$
May	Boston Symphony Orchestra: Opening Night at the Pops	$
May	Friends of the Public Garden: Ladies Garden Party	$$
May	Celebration of Women in Healthcare	$
May	Perkins School for the Blind Annual Gala	$$
May	Boston Chamber of Commerce Annual Meeting	$$
Spring	Boston Symphony Orchestra: Annual Presidents at the Pops	$$

KEY: $=$1-$100 $$=$100–$500 $$$=$500–$1000 $$$$=$1000+

Date		Price
June	Boston Business Journal: Best Places to Work	$
June	YWCA: Tribute to Outstanding Women	$$
June	Friends of the Public Garden: Green & White Ball	$$$
July	Boston Magazine's Best of Boston	by invite
July	American Ireland Fund Nantucket	$$$
July	French Library and Cultural Center: Bastille Day	$
September	Boston Business Journal:	
	Champions in Healthcare Awards	$
September	Black and White Boston: Black and White on a Green	
	Golf Tournament	$$
September	Jude Baker Children's Center: Annual Golf Tournament	
September/October		
	Boston Symphony Orchestra: Opening Night	$–$$$$
September	Joslin Regatta (Joslin Diabetes)	$$$$
September	Red Cross of Massachusetts Bay:	
	Women Who Care Breakfast	free
October	Boston Business Journal: 40 Under 40	$
September or October		
	New England Council Annual Dinner	
	(New Englander of the Year Award)	$$
October	The Commonwealth Institute: Breakfast for Champions	$
October	Girl Scouts Leading Women Awards	$$
October	Schwartz Center Annual Health Care Dinner	$$
October	United Way: Women's Leadership Breakfast	free
October	ROSE Fund: Annual Awards Dinner	$$
October	Rosie's Place: Funny Women...Serious Business	$$
October	MGH: Storybook Ball	$$$$
October	Jewish Family & Children's Service	
	of Greater Boston: Black Tie Gala	$$$
November	BIMDC Annual Fall Gala	$$
November	Colonel Daniel Marr Boys and Girls Club Annual Dinner	$$$
November	American Ireland Fund Gala Dinner	$$$
November	Children's Hospital Trust: Champions for Children's	$$$$
November	Health Law Advocates Breakfast	$$

Date		Price
November	Boston Foundation Annual Meeting	by invite
November	Chron's and Colitis Foundation of America: Annual Ball	$$
November	Dimock Community Health Center: Steppin' Out	$$
November	Big Sister Association: Big in Boston	$$
November/December		
	Children's Hospital Boston Festival	$$
December	Boston Chamber of Commerce Holiday Reception	$$
December	Boston Symphony Orchestra: Christmas at the Pops	$

Women's Award Events to Attend

Events that honor women are the best events to attend. Not only do you have a chance to rub elbows with the evening's leading lady, but you also can bet that the room will be filled with her Power Chick supporters and friends.

Abigail Adams Awards
Massachusetts Women's Political Caucus
JUNE
The Massachusetts Women's Political Caucus introduced the Tribute to Abigail Adams in 1988 to recognize six Massachusetts women leaders. Award recipients are women who have demonstrated through their work and/or their community activism an outstanding commitment to the realization of equal political, economic, and social rights for women.
www.mwpc.org

Academy of Women Achievers
YWCA
JUNE
The Academy of Women Achievers honors women who have demonstrated outstanding leadership and achievement in their professional and civic lives.
www.ywcaboston.org

Amelia Earhart Award
Crittenton Women's Union
SPRING
The Amelia Earhart Award was established in 1982 to recognize a woman who continues the pioneering spirit of Amelia Earhart and who has significantly contributed to the expansion of opportunities for women. The event, which benefits the Crittenton Women's Union, brings together a community of over 1,200 women and men.
www.liveworkthrive.org

Celebration of Women in Health Care
The Kennenth B. Schwartz Center
MAY

This increasingly popular event recognizes women for the key roles they play in healthcare and for their important contributions. It also offers a wonderful networking opportunity, and proceeds support the Schwartz Center's important programs. www.theschwartzcenter.org

New England Women's Leadership Awards
Colonel Daniel Marr Boys & Girls Club
MAY

The New England Women's Leadership Awards honor positive role models who inspire the young women of the Club to become leaders. Since its inception in 1992, nearly 70 women have been recognized in the fields of business, law, education, communications, health care, human services, politics, sports and the arts.
www.danmarrclub.org

Patriots' Trail Girl Scouts: Leading Women Award
Girl Scouts Patriots' Trail Council
OCTOBER

Each year the Patriots' Trail Girl Scout Council awards a leading and well respected woman in Boston. This fundraiser provides opportunities for the honorees, their organizations and other community leaders to support girls who will benefit from their experience, insight and financial support.
www.ptgirlscouts.org

Pinnacle Awards
Boston Chamber of Commerce
JANUARY

These annual awards honor professional women who have demonstrated excellence in entrepreneurship, management, and lifetime achievement. A highlight on the Chamber's annual calendar, The Pinnacle Award Luncheon is one of the Chamber's largest events, with more than 1,000 people in attendance. The honorees are women who have made strides in both their chosen fields and in the community.
www.bostonchamber.com

The Lelia J. Robinson Award
Women's Bar Association of Massachusetts
OCTOBER
Recent honorees include Sen. Hillary Rodham Clinton; former U.S. Attorney General Janet Reno; Maria Krokidas of Krokidas & Bluestein; Stephanie Page of the Committee for Public Counsel Services; Lauren Stiller Rikleen of Bowditch & Dewey; and Janet Donovan of Casa Myrna Vazquez, Inc.
www.womensbar.org

Wonder Woman Awards
Massachusetts Women's Political Caucus
JULY/AUGUST
The Wonder Women Awards honor women who work tirelessly behind the scenes in the political and nonprofit communities.
www.mwpc.org

Women of Valor Awards
Jewish Funds for Justice
APRIL
The Women of Valor Award celebrates the achievements of outstanding Jewish women who lead through their activism, accomplishments, philanthropy and commitment to social justice.
www.jfjustice.org

Women's Business: Hall of Fame
Women's Business
NOVEMBER
Each year Women's Business chooses four women, from over 200 nominees, who have an exceptional story that inspire other women in the business world. Women's Business chooses an executive, an entrepreneur, a professional and a "rising star" or women in a start up business to honor.
www.business.bostonherald.com/womensbusiness

Boards for Now

Many civic organizations are actively looking to re-energize their boards. The nonprofit community is engaged; any nonprofit is a great place to start. Here are a few we know well:

American Ireland Fund – The Young Leaders
211 Congress Street
Boston, MA 02110
(617) 574-0720
www.irlfunds.org
President and CEO: Kingsley Aikins
Regional Director: Bridget Hester
The American Ireland Fund is an international organization dedicated to raising funds and awareness in an effort to support programs throughout Ireland. The Young Leaders was established by a group of young Irish-American professionals who sought to connect with their heritage and pursue their vision of a stronger, more vibrant Ireland. The Young Leaders choose the causes they support and are committed to assisting projects that invest in Ireland's future, particularly charities that aid challenged youth and promote education and integration.

Animal Rescue League Boston
10 Chandler Street
Boston, MA 02116
(617) 426-9170
www.arlboston.org
President: Jay Bowen
The Animal Rescue League is a nonprofit organization committed to rescuing animals both domesticated and wild.

ArtsBoston
31 St. James Avenue, Suite 360
Boston, MA 02116
(617) 262-8632
www.artsboston.org
Executive Director: Catherine Peterson
ArtsBoston works to promote the arts in Greater Boston.

Boston Bar Association – New Lawyers Section
16 Beacon Street
Boston, MA 02108
(617) 742-0615
www.bostonbar.org
President: Jack Cinquegrana
The New Lawyers Section of the Boston Bar Association
assists attorneys of all ages in their first decade of practice.
Members practice in every professional setting and in every area
of law. The Section's activities include: social and networking
programs, cultural events, informal discussion series, CLE's, struc-
tured opportunities for pro bono service and other professional
development programs.

Boston Neighborhood Network
8 Park Plaza, Suite 2240
Boston, MA 02116
(617) 720-2113
www.bnntv.org
President: DeWayne Lehman
Boston Neighborhood Network acts as a public forum for
Boston residents, nonprofit and community-based organizations,
governmental and educational institutions. Members of the
BNN have access to three television studios, digital field
production and editing equipment, a multimedia lab, and a
mobile production truck.

BSA – Boston Society of Architects
52 Broad Street
Boston, MA 02109-4301
(617) 951-1433 x228
www.architects.org
President: Hubert Murray
The Boston Society of Architects administers programs and
resources that enhance the practice of architecture and the
public and professional understanding of design. The organization is dedicated to promoting the artistic, scientific and
administrative competence of the profession and encouraging
civic, educational and cultural activities.

Combined Jewish Philanthropies – Young Leadership Division
126 High Street
Boston, MA 02110
(617) 457-8565
www.cjp.org
President: Barry Shrage
The Young Leadership Division is dedicated to helping young professionals become involved in a broad range of educational, community service, philanthropic, and leadership development activities within the Jewish Community.

Friends of the Public Garden –
Young Friends of the Public Garden
87 Mount Vernon St.
Boston, MA 02108
(617) 723-8144
President: Henry Lee
www.friendsofthepublicgarden.org
The Friends of the Public Garden is a nonprofit citizen's advocacy group which was formed to work with the city to preserve and enhance the Boston Public Garden, Common, and Commonwealth Avenue Mall.

Girls Leap
25 River Street
Cambridge, MA 02139
(617) 441-2112
www.girlsleap.org
President of the Board of Directors: Stephanie Jordan Brown
LEAP Program Manager: Tracey Gridley
Girls Leap is dedicated to promoting the safety and well-being of girls, women, and their families in underserved communities through focused educational programs. The organization seeks to raise awareness in order to improve and create safer communities.

Institute of Contemporary Art – The New Group
100 Northern Avenue
Boston, MA 02210
(617) 478-3102
www.icaboston.org
President: Jill Medvedow
For more than a half century, the ICA has presented contemporary art in all media, visual arts, film, and video, performance and literature, and created educational programs that encourage an appreciation for contemporary culture. New Group members get a chance to experience Boston's lively contemporary art scene through an exciting series of social, educational, and fundraising events. New Group members also receive discounts on tickets and invitations to special events hosted by other local arts organizations.

MSPCA
350 South Huntington Avenue
Boston, MA 02130
(617) 522-7400
www.mspca.org
President: Dana Ramish
Head of the Board of Directors: Robert Cummings
Head of the Board of Overseers: Carolyn Ross
The second-oldest humane society in the United States, MSPCA is a national and international leader in animal protection and veterinary medicine. The MSPCA is devoted to providing animal protection and adoption, advocacy, humane education, law enforcement and the highest-quality veterinary care.

MSPCC – Boston Metro Professionals Board
99 Summer Street
Boston, MA 02115
(617) 587-1505
www.mspcc.org
President and CEO: Marylou Sudders
Chairman of the Board of Directors: Stephen G. Pagliuca
MSPCC is a private, nonprofit society dedicated to protecting
and promoting the rights and well being of children and families.

NAIOP – Future Leaders (NFL) committee
144 Gould Street, Suite 140
Needham, MA 02494
(781) 453-6900
www.naiopma.org
President of the Executive Committee: Jay Doherty
NAIOP is the international association of developers, owners
and professionals of commercial, industrial and mixed-use real
estate. The Future Leaders committee was formed as a way to
develop future chapter leadership and is open to all members
who are age 35 and under.

ONEin3 Boston
Boston Redevelopment Authority
One City Hall Square
Boston, MA 02201
(617) 918-4303
www.onein3boston.org
Manager: Devin Cole
Board of Directors Chair: Andrea Lang
ONEin3 Boston seeks to serve the one-third of Boston's
population that is between the ages of 20 and 34. The
program works to connect Boston's young adults with resources
related to home buying, business development, professional
networking, and civic engagement.

Rosie's Place
889 Harrison Avenue
Boston, MA 02118
(617) 442-9322
www.rosies.org
Executive Director: Sue Marsh
Chair of the Board of Directors: Michele May
Rosie's Place is devoted to providing a safe and nurturing environment for poor and homeless women. Since 1974, Rosie's Place has worked endlessly to help homeless women maintain their dignity, seek opportunity and find security in their lives.

Save the Harbor / Save the Bay
Boston Fish Pier
212 Northern Avenue, Suite 304 West
Boston, MA 02210
(617) 451-2860
www.savetheharbor.org
President: Patricia A. Foley
Board of Directors: Beth Nicholson
Save the Harbor/Save the Bay is a non profit public interest harbor advocacy organization. The organization is made up of thousands of citizens, as well as scientists, and civic, corporate, cultural and community leaders whose mission is to restore and protect Boston Harbor, Massachusetts Bay, and the marine environment.

United Way of Massachusetts Bay – Young Professionals
51 Sleeper Street
Boston, MA 02210
(617) 624-8000
www.uwmb.org
Interim President: Mary Kay Leonard
Chairman of the Executive Committee: Robert M. Mahoney
United Way's Young Leaders Program provides community involvement and personal development opportunities for "up and coming" philanthropic young professionals, ages 21 to 40, who come together from across the community to provide volunteer leadership and management skills to improve lives and strengthen our region, making it the best place for children in the country.

Urban League of Eastern Massachusetts –
Young Professionals Network
88 Warren Street
Roxbury, MA 02119
(617) 442 4519 x 255
www.ypnboston.org
President and CEO: Darnell Williams
Chairman of the Board: Richard Taylor
President of the Young Professionals Network:
Duane Johnson
Young Professionals Network is an auxiliary of the Urban
League of Eastern Massachusetts. The group is comprised of
young Black professionals (ages 21 to 40) in Boston who
provide leadership development and advancement, economic
empowerment and community volunteer opportunities for other
young professionals. The organization trains and educates young
professionals so they may take leadership roles within the
National Urban League, Fortune 500 companies, and society
at large.

Young Nonprofit Professionals Network – Boston Chapter
http://lincboston.org/
The Young Nonprofit Professionals Network promotes an effi-
cient nonprofit sector that supports the growth, learning, and
development of young professionals.

Boards for Tomorrow

Of course, in business, obtaining a seat on a corporate board represents the pinnacle of success. Here, we're more focused on the civic and charitable circles. For more information about corporate boards, refer to the Boston Club, www.thebostonclub.com.

Education

Corporate boards aside, higher education and healthcare are at the top of the food chain, particularly if it's MIT, Harvard, or Boston College. You know the most prestigious names. The majority of these seats are cultivated by individuals already sitting on the board, or by the organization's management. However, any university or college is worth your time if you have the opportunity.

Hospitals

Some of the best medical care and academic hospital facilities in the world are found here in Boston and the surrounding communities. Academic medical centers are key drivers of the economy and innovation; however, community hospitals are also very important. All possess high-level, coveted board seats.

Museums and Cultural Organizations

Boston Ballet
19 Clarendon Street
Boston, MA 02116-6100
(617) 695-6950
www.bostonballet.org
Boston Ballet's mission is to bring new levels of excellence to ballet, both on and offstage, and to significantly advance ballet as an art form to enrich the cultural life of the community.

Boston Symphony Orchestra

301 Massachusetts Avenue
Boston, MA 02115
(617) 266-1492
www.bso.org
Chairman: Ed Linde
Managing Director: Mark Volpe
Boston Symphony Orchestra is one of the most prominent
art organizations in the country. The Boston Symphony
Orchestra both educates and entertains music lovers of all ages,
throughout Boston.

Citi Performing Arts Center

270 Tremont Street
Boston, MA 02116
(617) 482-9393
www.wangcenter.org
President and CEO: Josiah A. Spaulding, Jr.
Citi Performing Arts Center (formerly The Wang Center for the
Performing Arts, Inc.) is a non-profit organization dedicated to
presenting broad-based, popular art and entertainment. The
organization also offers arts education programming that is accessible to adults, youth and families throughout greater Boston.

Isabella Stewart Gardner Museum

280 The Fenway
Boston, MA 02115
(617) 566-1401
www.gardnermuseum.org
President: Anne Hawley
For over 100 years the Isabella Stewart Gardner Museum has
been viewed as one of the nation's finest collections of art. The
museum features three floors of galleries with art spanning 30
centuries and is surrounded by a garden courtyard.

Institute of Contemporary Art
100 Northern Avenue
Boston, MA 02210
(617) 478-3100
www.icaboston.org
Director: Jill Medvedow
For more than a half century, the ICA has presented contemporary art in all media, visual arts, film, and video, performance and literature, and created educational programs that encourage an appreciation for contemporary culture.

Museum of Fine Arts
465 Huntington Avenue
Boston, MA 02115-5597
(617) 267-9300
www.mfa.org
Director: Malcolm Rogers
The Museum of Fine Arts houses and preserves preeminent collections of art.

New Center for Arts and Culture
18 Tremont Street, Suite 308
Boston, MA 02108
(617) 965-0352
www.ncacboston.org
Executive Director and CEO: Daniel Neuman
The New Center for Arts and Culture is devoted to exploring societal change through art and culture. The New Center attracts intellectual and cultural leaders from Boston and around the world to guide the development of its exhibitions and programs.

Human Services

American Red Cross of Massachusetts Bay
139 Main Street
Cambridge, MA 02142
(617) 274-5200
www.bostonredcross.org
President and CEO: Deborah Jackson
Chair: Nancy Leaming
Vice Chair: Geri Denterlein
The local chapter of this renowned organization is a leader in disaster response, health and safety, international services, training and hunger relief.

Big Brothers Big Sisters of Massachusetts Bay
75 Federal Street, 5th Floor
Boston, MA 02110
(617) 542-9090
www.bbmb.org
President and CEO: Judy Vredenburgh
President of the Board of Directors: Jerry Martinson
Big Brother and Big Sister Association is dedicated to helping children reach their full potential. Through matched one-on-one relationships, volunteer mentors positively impact the lives of young children across the country.

Boys & Girls Clubs of Boston
50 Congress Street, Suite 730
Boston, MA 02109
617 994-4700
www.bgcb.org
President and CEO: Linda Whitlock
Chair of the Board: Sandra M. Edgerley
The Boys and Girls Club is devoted to helping all young people reach their full potential as productive, caring, responsible citizens. The Boys & Girls Club also offers programs and services that promote and enhance the development of boys and girls by instilling a sense of competence, usefulness, belonging and influence.

Combined Jewish Philanthropies
126 High Street
Boston, MA 02110
(617) 457-8500
www.cjp.org
President: Barry Shrage
Combined Jewish Philanthropies is the country's oldest
Federated Jewish philanthropy. CJP has come together over
generations to take care of people in need, both here in Boston
and around the world.

Crittenton Women's Union
One Washington Mall
Boston, MA 02108
(617) 259-2900
www.liveworkthrive.org
President and CEO: Elizabeth Babcock
Chair of the Board of Directors: Francene Sussner Rodgers
The Crittenton Women's Union works to assist women in need
so that they can attain economic independence and create
better futures for themselves and their families.

Greater Boston Food Bank
99 Atkinson Street
Boston, MA 02118
(617) 427-5200
www.bgfb.org
President and CEO: Catherine D'Amato
Chair of the Executive Committee: Vicary M. Graham
The Greater Boston Food Bank is the largest hunger-relief organization in New England, and one of the largest food banks in
the country, serving 190 communities in eastern Massachusetts.

MSPCC
Massachusetts Society for the Prevention of Cruelty to Children
99 Summer Street
Boston, MA 02110
(617) 587-1500
www.mspcc.org
President and CEO: Marylou Sudders
Chair of the Board of Directors: Stephen G. Pagliuca
MSPCC is a private, nonprofit organization devoted to strengthening families and preventing child abuse through essential child welfare, mental health treatment and effective public advocacy. MSPCC serves children and families across Massachusetts with a range of services designed to respond to the individual needs of infants, children, adolescents and their families.

New England Home for Little Wanderers
271 Huntington Avenue
Boston, MA 02115
(617) 267-3700
www.thehome.org
President and CEO: Joan Wallace-Benjamin
Chairman of the Board of Directors: John Thomas Hailer
The Home for Little Wanderers is a nationally renowned, private, nonprofit child and family service agency. The mission of the Home is to ensure the healthy emotional, mental, and social development of children, families, and communities at risk.

The Steppingstone Foundation
77 Summer St
Boston, MA 02110
(617) 423-6300
www.tsf.org
Executive Management: Michael Danziger
Director of the Board of Directors: Amy Smith Berylson
The Steppingstone Foundation is a nonprofit organization that creates programs that prepare urban school children for educational opportunities that lead to college. Steppingstone programs emphasize rigorous standards and achieve meaningful results.

United Way of Massachusetts Bay
51 Sleeper Street
Boston, MA 02210
(617) 624.8000
www.uwmb.org
Interim President: Mary Kay Leonard
Chairman of the Board: Robert M. Mahoney
United Way of Massachusetts Bay is a locally run chapter of
the United Way of America. UWMB is one of the largest
United Way organizations, serving 64 cities and towns across
Eastern Massachusetts, and supporting a network of 259 non-
profit agencies.

General nonprofit

WGBH
PO Box 200
Boston, MA 02134
(617) 300-5400
www.wgbh.org
WGBH produces shows throughout the state that educate
and entertain audiences of all ages.

WBUR
890 Commonwealth Avenue, 3rd Floor
Boston, MA 02215
(617) 353-0909
www.wbur.org
WBUR, a premiere public radio station, provides local, national
and international news, as well as reports and programs from
National Public Radio.

YMCA of Greater Boston
316 Huntington Avenue
Boston, MA 02115
(617) 536-6950
www.ymcaboston.org
President and CEO: John M. Ferrell
The YMCA, dedicated to providing affordable and accessible
programs for families and youth, provides child care, after-school
programming, job training and English as a Second Language
courses to thousands of local residents each year.

The Boston Foundation
75 Arlington Street
Boston, MA 02116
(617) 338-1700
www.tbf.org
President: Paul Grogan
Chair of the Board of Directors: Reverend Ray Hammond
The Boston Foundation is dedicated to building and sustaining
a vital, prosperous city and region, where justice and opportunity are extended to everyone. The Foundation is considered a
convener and works with other organizations to find new ways
to explore important issues and to strengthen communities.

Women's Organizations

American Association of University Women of Massachusetts
(617) 327-0448
www.aauw-ma.org

Association of Women in Science
Abbott Bioresearch Center
100 Research Drive
Worcester, MA 01605
(508) 849-2655
www.awis.org

Boston Chamber of Commerce – Women's Network
75 State Street, 2nd Floor
Boston, MA 02109
(617) 227-4500
www.bostonchamber.com/

Boston Club
P. O. Box 1126
Marblehead, MA 01945
(781) 639-8002
www.thebostonclub.com/

Boston Women Communicators
P.O. Box 404
Back Bay Station
Boston, MA 02117
(617) 723-5642

Boston Women's Commission
Room 716
1 City Hall Plaza
Boston, MA 02201
(617) 635-3138
www.cityofboston.gov/women

Boston Women's Network
(617) 723-5642
bwc94@verizon.net
www.bostonwomensnetwork.org

Boston Women's Fund
14 Beacon Street
Suite 805
Boston, MA 02108
(617) 725-0035
www.bostonwomensfund.org

Center for Women in Enterprise
24 School Street
Suite 700
Boston MA 02108
(617) 536-0700
www.cweboston.org

Commonwealth Institute
10 High Street, Suite 1002
Boston, MA 02110
(617) 859-0080
www.commonwealthinstitute.org

Massachusetts Commission on the Status of Women
The Charles F. Hurley Building
19 Staniford St., 6th Floor
Boston, MA 02114-2502
(617) 626-6520
www.mass.gov/women

Massachusetts Women's Political Caucus
11 Beacon Street Suite 432
Boston, MA 02108
(617) 451-9294
www.mwpc.org

MassNOW
1105 Commonwealth Avenue, Suite 201
Boston, MA 02215
(617) 254-9130
http://www.massnow.org

New England Women Business Owners
P.O. Box 67082
Chestnut Hill, MA 02467-0001
(617) 566-3013
http://www.newbo.org

New England Women In Real Estate
c/o Harron & Associates
229 Berkeley Street
Boston MA 02116
(617) 247-2346
www.newire.org

**The Alliance of Women's Business
and Professional Organizations**
P.O. Box 67183
Chestnut Hill, MA 02467
(617) 277-3304
info@womensalliance.org
www.womensalliance.org

The College Club
44 Commonwealth Avenue
Boston, MA 02116
(617) 536-9510

Massachusetts Women's Forum
c /o CMT Entertainment
9B Hamilton Place, 4th Floor
Boston, MA 02108
(617) 357-0032
mwf@cmtentertainment.com

Women in Development of Greater Boston
93 Concord Avenue, Suite 2
Belmont, MA 02478
(617) 489-6777
www.widgb.org

Women in Health Care Management
84 Fenwick Road
Newton, MA 02468
www.whcm.org

Women's Bar Association of Massachusetts
18 Tremont Street, Suite 730
Boston, MA 02108
(617) 973-6666
www.womensbar.org

Women's Caucus for Art (Boston Chapter)
(617) 445-2648
www.wcaboston.org

Power Dining

This list is an amalgam of our top picks and those recognized by Boston's press and women leaders.

Abe & Louie's
793 Boylston Street
Boston, MA 02116
(617) 536-6300
www.abeandlouies.com
Cuisine: American, Steakhouse, Seafood
Features: Fireplace Seating, Full Bar, Extensive Wine List

Brasserie Jo
120 Huntington Avenue
Boston, MA 02116
(617) 351-2071
www.colonnadehotel.com
Cuisine: French
Features: Breakfast and Brunch Menu, Private Dining,
Notable Wine List

Bristol Lounge
The Four Seasons
200 Boylston Street
Boston, MA 02116
(617) 351-2071
www.fourseasons.com
Cuisine: Contemporary
Features: Heart-healthy Dishes, Full Bar, Entertainment

Blu
The Sports Club/ LA
4 Avery Street
Boston MA 02111
(617) 375-8550
www.blurestaurant.com
Cuisine: Contemporary
Features: Full Bar, Extensive Wine List, Heart-healthy Dishes,
Celebrity Hotspot

Café Fleuri
Langham Hotel Boston
250 Franklin Street
Boston, MA 02110
(617) 451-1900
www.langhamhotels.com
Cuisine: Mediterranean
Features: Numerous awards, Saturday Chocolate Bar
and Sunday Jazz Brunch

Capital Grille
359 Newbury Street
Boston, MA 02115
(617) 262-8900
www.thecapitalgrille.com
Cuisine: American, Steakhouse, Seafood
Features: Fulll Bar and Menu Extensive Wine List, Private Dining,
Celebrity Hotspot

Clio
Elliot Hotel
370 Commonwealth Avenue
Boston, MA 02215
(617) 356-7200
www.cliorestaurant.com
Cuisine: French, Contemporary
Features: Numerous Awards, Brunch Menu, Elegant Private Dining

Eastern Standard
Hotel Commonwealth
528 Commonwealth Ave
Boston, MA 02215
(617) 532-9100
www.hotelcommonwealth.com
Cuisine: American, Seafood
Features: Full Bar and Menu, Breakfast Menu, Private Dining Rooms

Grill 23 & Bar
161 Berkeley Street
Boston, MA 02116
(617) 542-2255
www.grill23.com
Cuisine: Steakhouse, Seafood
Features: Full Bar, Great Wine List, Private Dining Rooms

Henrietta's Table
The Charles Hotel
One Bennett Street
Cambridge, MA 02138
(617) 661-5005
www.henriettastable.com
Cuisine: Vegetarian
Features: Breakfast Menu, Causal Dining Area, Good Wine List

Johnny's Luncheonette
30 Langley Rd
Newton, MA 02459-1918
(617) 527-3223
Cuisine: American
Features: Old-Fashion Diner Feel, Breakfast Menu

Locke-Ober
3 Winterplace
Boston, MA 02108
(617) 542-1340
www.locke-ober.com
Cuisine: French, Seafood
Features: Full Bar, Lounge, Multiple Private Rooms

Mistral
223 Columbus Avenue
Boston, MA 02116
(617) 867-9300
www.mistralbistro.com
Cuisine: French Mediterranean
Feature: Full Bar, Private Dinning Room (Le Salon du Mistral),
Seasonal Menu

No. 9 Park
9 Park Street
Boston, MA 02108
(617) 742-9991
www.no9park.com
Cuisine: Contemporary/International
Feature: Private Dining, Notable Wine List

Radius
8 High Street
Boston, MA 02110
(617) 426-1234
www.radiusrestaurant.com
Cuisine: French, Contemporary
Features: Extensive Wine List, Heart-Healthy Dishes, Full Bar,
Private Rooms

Taj Bar
15 Arlington Street
Boston, MA 02116
(617) 536-5700
www.tajhotels.com
Features: Award-Winning Martinis, Fireplace and a View of
the Public Garden

Upstairs on the Square
91 Winthrop Street
Cambridge, MA 02138
(617) 864-1933
www.upstairsonthesquare.com
Cuisine: American, Seafood
Features: Private Dining Room, Extensive Wine List, Full Bar,
Fireside Dining

Pinnacle Award Winners
Boston Chamber of Commerce

2007 Pinnacle Awards

Achievement in Entrepreneurship
Anne Bailey Berman, president and CEO,
Chadwick Martin Bailey

Achievement in Management, Private Sector
Joanne Jaxtimer, SVP, director of corporate affairs
Mellon Financial Corporation

Achievement in Management, Government
Stephanie Lovell, first assistant Attorney General
Commonwealth of Massachusetts

Achievement in Management, Non-Profit
Sandra Fenwick, chief operating officer
Children's Hospital Boston;

Achievement in the Professions
Michele Whitham, co-managing partner
Foley Hoag LLP

Achievement in Arts & Education
Marita Rivero, VP & general manager
WGBH

Emerging Executive
Melissa Palmer, senior manager
PricewaterhouseCoopers LLP

Lifetime Achievement
Swanee Hunt, president
Hunt Alternatives Fund.

2006 Pinnacle Awards
Achievement in Entrepreneurship
Donna Latson Gittens, Founder and CEO
causemedia, inc.

Achievement in Management – Private Sector
Cheryl A. LaFleur, President, New England Distribution
National Grid

Achievement in Management - Government
Kathleen M. O'Toole, Police Commissioner
Boston Police Department

Achievement in Management – Non-Profit
JudyAnn Bigby, M.D., Medical Director, Community Health Programs
Brigham and Women's Hospital

Achievement in the Professions
Marianne Ajemian, Esq., Partner
Nutter McClennen & Fish LLP

Achievement in Arts & Education
Libbie J. Shufro, President and CEO
Boston Center for the Arts

Emerging Executive
Julie Anne Smith, Vice President, Global Marketing
Genzyme Corporation

Lifetime Achievement
Cathy Minehan, President and CEO
Federal Reserve Bank of Boston

2005 Pinnacle Awards
Achievement in Entrepreneurship
Maryanne Cataldo, CEO & Founder
City Lights Electrical Company, Inc.

Achievement in Management – Private Sector
Donna C. Cupelo, Region President – Massachusetts & Rhode
IslandVerizon Communications

Achievement in Management – Government
Barbara J. Boylan, Director of Design
Massachusetts Bay Transportation Authority

Achievement in Management – Non-Profit
Joan Wallace-Benjamin, Ph.D.
President & CEO

The Home for Little Wanderers
Achievement in Arts & Education
Jill Medvedow, James Sachs Plaut Director

The Institute for Contemporary Art
Emerging Executive
Zamawa Arenas, Principal ARGUS

Lifetime Achievement
Marion L. Heard, President & CEO
Oxen Hill Partners

2004 Pinnacle Awards
Achievement in Entrepreneurship
Pamela G. McDermott, Founder and President
McDermott Ventures, LLC

Achievement in Management – Private Sector
Heather P. Campion, Group Executive Vice President and
Director of Corporate Affairs
Citizens Financial Group, Inc.

Achievement in Management – Government
Middlesex District Attorney Martha Coakley

Achievement in Management – Non-Profit
Jeraldine (Jerry) Martinson, Executive Director
Big Sister Association of Greater Boston

Excellence in Arts & Education
Sister Janet Eisner, SND, President
Emmanuel College

Emerging Executive
Noriko Miyakoda Hall, Vice President
Tishman Construction Corporation of New England

Lifetime Achievement
Jackie Jenkins-Scott, President and CEO
Dimock Community Health Center

2003 Pinnacle Awards

Achievement in Business
Joan N. Gardner, President
Applied Geographics, Inc.

Achievement in Management – Private Sector
Anne Finucane, Director and Executive Vice President,
Corporate Marketing and Communications
FleetBoston Financial

Achievement in Management – Non-Profit
Deborah C. Jackson, CEO
American Red Cross of Massachusetts Bay

Emerging Executive
Andrea C. Silbert, Founder & CEO
Center for Women & Enterprise

Lifetime Achievement
Benaree P. Wiley, President & CEO
The Partnership, Inc.

2002 Pinnacle Awards

Achievement in Business
Vicki Donlan, CEO, Founder, Owner, Publisher
Women@s Business LLC

Achievement in Management   Private Sector
Karen Kaplan, President, Boston Office
Hill, Holliday, Connors, Cosmopulos, Inc.
(now Hill | Holiday)

Achievement in Management   Government
Charlotte Golar Richie, Chief of Housing, City of Boston
Director, Department of Neighborhood Development

Achievement in Management   Non Profit
Charlayne Murrell Smith, Vice President, External Relations
The Children's Museum

Achievement in the Professions
Dale Rogers Marshall, President
Wheaton College

Emerging Executive
Lisa A. Brothers, Vice President & COO
Judith Nitsch Engineering, Inc.

Lifetime Achievement
Elaine Ullian, President & CEO
Boston Medical Center

2001 Pinnacle Awards

Achievement in Business
Harron Ellenson, President
Harron & Associates

Achievement in Management   Private Sector
Gayle B. Farris, President
Forest City Enterprises Boston

Achievement in Management   Government
Merita A. Hopkins, Corporation Counsel
City of Boston

Achievement in Management   Non Profit
Elizabeth G. Reilinger, Ph.D., President & CEO
Crittenton Hastings House

Achievement in the Professions
Regina M. Pisa, Chairman & Managing Partner
Goodwin, Procter & Hoar LLP

Emerging Executive
Karyn M. Wilson, Vice President of Marketing
ZEFER Corporation

Lifetime Achievement
Anna Faith Jones, President & CEO
The Boston Foundation

2000 Pinnacle Awards
Achievement in Business
Patricia Arredondo, President
Empowerment Workshops

Achievement in Management   Private Sector
Geri Denterlein, President
Denterlein Worldwide

Achievement in Management   Government
Lucy V. Shorter, Director Marketing Communications
MBTA

Achievement in Management Non Profit Sector
Ellen M. Zane, Network President
Partners HealthCare System, Inc.

Achievement in the Professions
Diane Hobbs, Partner
Nutter, McClennen & Fish, LLP

Emerging Executive
Carol Fulp, Second Vice President Community Relations
John Hancock Financial Services

Lifetime Achievement
Micho F. Spring, President & Partner
BSMG Worldwide

Selected Organizations
that make a Difference

Many civic and trade organizations make a difference in this city, here are a few of the most recognizable and influential:

Civic Organizations

A Better City
75 State St.
Boston, MA 02109
(617) 227-4500
www.abettercity.org

Greater Boston Chamber of Commerce
75 State Street, 2nd Floor
Boston, MA 02109
(617) 227-4500
www.bostonchamber.com/

Massachusetts Taxpayers Foundation
333 Washington Street, Suite 853
Boston, MA 02108
(617) 720-1000
www.masstaxpayers.org

AIM (Associated Industries of Massachusetts)
22 Berkeley Street
P.O. Box 763
Boston, MA 02117-0763
(617) 262-1180
www.aimnet.org

Massachusetts Business Roundtable
141 Tremont Street
Boston, MA 02111
(617) 728-0881
www.maroundtable.com

MA Biotech Council
One Cambridge Center
Cambridge, MA 02142
(617) 674-5100
www.massbio.org

MA High Tech Council
Reservoir Place
1601 Trapelo Road, Suite 336
Waltham, MA 02451
(781) 890-6482
www.mhtc.org/
www.masshightechconcil@mhtc.org

Boston Municipal Research Bureau
333 Washington Street, Suite 854
Boston, MA 02108
(617) 227-1900
www.bmrb.org/

Boston Foundation
75 Arlington Street, 10th floor
Boston, MA 02116
(617) 338-1700
www.tbf.org

MassInc
18 Tremont Street, Suite 1120
Boston, MA 02108
(617) 742-6800
www.massinc.org

Legal
Boston Bar Association
6 Beacon Street
Boston, MA 02108
(617) 742.0615
www.bostonbar.org

Massachusetts Bar Association
20 West Street
Boston, MA 02111-1204
(617) 338-0500
www.massbar.org/

Women's Bar Association
18 Tremont Street, Suite 730
Boston, MA 02108
(617) 973-6666
www.womensbar.org/WBA

Real Estate

Boston Society of Architects
52 Broad Street
Boston, MA 02109-4301
(617) 951-1433
www.architects.org/

NAIOP
144 Gould Street, Suite 140
Needham, MA 02494
(781) 453-6900
www.naiopma.org/

NEWIRE
229 Berkeley Street
Boston MA 02116
(617) 247-2346
www.newire.org

Urban Land Institute – Boston
37 Milk Street, Suite 705
Boston, MA 02109
(617) 938-6468
www.uli.org/

Accounting

MA Society of CPAs
105 Chauncy Street, 10th Floor
Boston, MA 02111
(617) 556-4000
www.mscpaonline.org/

High Tech/BioTech

Mass Biotech
One Cambridge Center
Cambridge, MA 02142
(617) 674-5100
www.massbio.org/

Mass Medic
715 Albany Street, TW1
Boston, MA 02118
(617) 414-1340
www.massmedic.com/

Massachusetts Software Council
One Exeter Plaza
Boston MA 02116
(617) 437-0600
www.masstlc.org/

Additional Resources

Organizations

Boston Chamber of Commerce
Boston's Future Leaders
75 State Street, 2nd Floor
Boston, MA 02109
(617) 227-4500
www.bostonchamber.com

Boston Center for Community & Justice (LeadBoston)
38 Chauncy Street, Suite 812
Boston, MA 02111
(617) 451-5010
www.bostonccj.org

Center for Women in Enterprise
24 School Street, Suite 700
Boston, MA 02108
(617) 536-0700
www.cweonline.org

Center for Women's Leadership – Babson College
Babson College
Center for Women's Leadership
Babson Park, MA 02457-0310
(781) 239-5001
www3.babson.edu/cwl

Connect & Serve
Massachusetts Volunteerism
Check out this online searchable database of hundreds of volunteer
opportunities, provided by the Commonwealth of Massachusetts.
www.volunteersolutions.org/mass-service/volunteer/home

Women's Network
Boston Chamber of Commerce
www.bostonchamber.com/programs/womensnetwork.asp

Simmons School of Management, Executive Education
409 Commonwealth Avenue
Boston, MA 02215
(617) 521-3869
www.simmons.edu/som/execed

The Partnership, Inc.
545 Boyleston Street, 3rd Floor
Boston, MA 02116
(617) 262-2828
www.thepartnership.com

UMass Emerging Leaders Program
100 Morrissey Boulevard
Boston, MA 02125-3393
(617) 287-5000
www.leaders.umb.edu/index.html